# THE MAGNOLIA STORY

# THE MAGNOLIA STORY

## CHIP & JOANNA GAINES

with Mark Dagostino

W PUBLISHING GROUP

AN IMPRINT OF THOMAS NELSON

Published in Nashville, Tennessee, by W Publishing, an imprint of Thomas Nelson. W Publishing and Thomas Nelson are registered trademarks of HarperCollins Christian Publishing, Inc.

Thomas Nelson titles may be purchased in bulk for educational, business, fund-raising, or sales promotional use. For information, please e-mail SpecialMarkets@ ThomasNelson.com.

**Library of Congress Control Number: 2016945748**

ISBN 9780718079185

*Printed in the United States of America*

18 19 20 21   LSC   25 24 23

*We would like to dedicate this book to our children—Drake, Ella Rose, Emmie Kay, and Duke—and to the children of Restoration Gateway. Our commitment to you will never fade.*

# CONTENTS

# BLESSINGS IN
# (A BIG, UGLY) DISGUISE

I have always been one to play it safe. If it were up to me, the less risk involved the better. But this isn't how the story goes—because I am married to the one, the only, Chip Carter Gaines.

One day back in early 2012, my husband decided to go window-shopping online. That's always a risky thing to do, but when Chip's the man behind the mouse it can be downright dangerous. I never know what object—or animal—might show up at my front door on the back of some random delivery truck.

On this particular day, Chip happened to spot a used houseboat for sale.

We'd been living in a house that we were getting ready to flip and we'd just started renovating our farmhouse outside of Waco, Texas, which meant we were on the hunt for a temporary place to live. So Chip clicked through the pictures of that floating two-story shanty with its microscopic kitchen and had a full-blown Chip Gaines epiphany.

I really thought to myself, *How cool would it be to move our family onto a houseboat? We can put it on one of the lakes down here, and the kids and I can fish for breakfast from the balcony. Wow! Jo's gonna love this.*

So he bought it. Sight unseen. We just barely had our heads above water at that point, and he went and threw tens of thousands of dollars down on that thing. And then he didn't say a word. He had it shipped to Waco on a monster tractor-trailer and couldn't wait to show off his surprise when it finally arrived. After all our years of marriage, he was still clueless about how I might react.

I had no idea any of this was going on, of course. But right around that same time, on some random weeknight, I received a phone call from an out-of-state number I didn't recognize. I picked it up.

"Hi, I'm Katie Neff, and I work for a television production company," the woman on the line said. "I saw some of your designs online, and I was wondering . . ."

This Katie had apparently seen photos of our most recent flip house that I'd designed, the one we were living in at the time. A few weeks earlier a friend of mine, Molly, had submitted those photos to a popular blog called DesignMom.com, and I'd been excited that a blog with thousands of followers wanted to feature it. It was the first time my work had ever really been featured on a design blog other than my own. I had a loyal local following back then, but no national following to speak of.

"I loved what you did," Katie continued, "so I looked you up and read *your* blog too. I see that you and your husband work together, and I was just wondering: Would you ever want to be on a TV show?"

I sat there and thought, *Did I just hear that right?*

"What about us would you want to show on TV?" I asked.

"Well, we just love how organic it is—that you and your husband work together. Not only do you sell homes, but you also flip and renovate them. We think it's unique that you're a husband-and-wife team." She went on and on, and I finally said, "Well, let me talk to Chip and I'll get back with you."

I got with Chip, and he immediately said, "That's a scam. Don't call them back."

I was just skeptical. Back in high school I had some buddies who were always trying to get into modeling. They would go to these "agents" and "casting calls" and then wind up paying some guy $1,000 to take their headshots, and nothing would ever come of it. So, yeah, I thought it was something like that.

Jo really thought we should give them a shot, but I was just like, "Jo, I'm telling you, there's no way this is legit. We're gonna meet these people, and they'll get us all excited thinking they're gonna make us famous or something, and then say, 'Oh, by the way, you need to pay us twenty grand.'"

I somehow convinced Chip to let me call Katie back. We didn't have a lot of money just lying around, so I knew there was no way anyone could trick us out of thousands of dollars. (Of course, I knew nothing about that houseboat yet!)

Sure enough, within a couple of weeks Katie sent an entire camera crew to Waco to spend five days filming us for what they called a "sizzle reel"—basically an extended commercial they would put together to try to sell a television series based on the two of us and our little business. They never asked us for any money at all. They were legit, which made us wonder: Why in the world would anyone care to watch us on TV? We don't even *watch* TV. These people have to be nuts.

After the crew spent a couple of days with us, they started thinking they might be nuts too. Chip and I were *horrible*. We were scared of the cameras, which is hilarious because Chip is the most talkative guy I know. But like clockwork, the moment that red light turned on, he froze.

My mouth was all dry and I couldn't think straight, and Jo was a little dull. They just followed Jo around and tried to make something out of nothing. It was pretty obvious this could not make good television. We were just awful. We really were.

The crew had me stand in my kitchen and try to make pancakes with the kids hanging off of my legs while Chip was basically sucking his thumb over in the corner, and the whole time I was trying to convince the kids not to look into the camera so it would look more "natural." It certainly didn't *feel* natural, and it definitely wasn't any fun.

On the fourth day, just before the camera crew was scheduled to go home, their top guy pulled us aside and said, "Look, if something doesn't happen here, there's no way you guys are getting a show. This just isn't working."

We figured we were pretty much done at that point, and it didn't really bother us at all. The two of us had never imagined we'd be on TV. We'd talked to friends about the kinds of things they watched on "reality TV," and from what we could tell, none of it seemed like us anyway.

Then something happened. The very next morning, the houseboat arrived. With cameras rolling, Chip put a blindfold on me and drove me to an empty lot by the lake.

With all cameras on me, Chip released the blindfold and said, "Ta-da!"

I wasn't sure what I was looking at. A shipwreck, maybe? On the back of a semi?

"What is that?" I said.

"I got this for you, Jo!" Chip replied.

"That *better* not be for me," I said. It was the ugliest, rundown-looking, two-story shack of a boat I'd ever seen. "What the heck are we going to do with a houseboat?"

"That's our new home!" Chip said, beaming with pride at his purchase.

"What? You are crazy. We are not living on a houseboat."

It quickly dawned on me that this wasn't a joke and Chip wasn't even close to kidding. I wasn't mishearing him. He was dead serious about making that boat our home for the next six months.

I just about lost it. "How can we live on the water, Chip? Three of our kids don't even know how to swim! Did you think this through?!"

Then he fessed up and told me how much money he'd spent on it. As it all sank in, I realized I'd never been so mad at him—ever—and that's saying something.

"Come on. At least come look at it. I know this can work," he pleaded.

As soon as we walked a little closer, we could see the holes. *Holes.* In the *boat.*

We pulled ourselves up onto the flatbed and went inside to find the interior covered in mold. Someone had taken the AC unit out on top and left a gaping hole in the roof, so for years it had rained straight into the boat. We tried turning the engine over, and of course it didn't start. That's when Chip got angry. "I think I got scammed," he said.

"Chip, did you even look at this thing before you bought it?"

"Well, no," he said. "It was a great deal, and there were all kinds of pictures. It looked like it was in great shape. Oh, wait a minute. I bet the guy just put up pictures of this thing from when he bought it, like in 1980 or something. That sorry sucker."

"Sorry sucker? Chip . . ."

By this point I'm trying to decide if we could scrap it for parts. My husband had made plenty of impulsive purchases. That's just what he does. He'd gone and purchased the house we were currently in without showing that to me, either. But at least it was a house, with a roof, on a foundation. I'd gone along with it, as I always do, and over time I'd come to love that quirky shoe box of a house.

We had worked hard to make it our home. In fact, that house is where I'd had my epiphany about truly owning the space you're in (a moment I'll share with you later in this book) and where I'd designed the kids' rooms that landed on the blog and caused the producer to call. I was already pretty upset that we were going to have to leave that house behind in a few months. But to think that we might have to move into this . . . *thing* was just too much.

"You need to return it," I said.

"It's paid for," Chip said. "It's done. I bought it as is."

"Excuse me, semi driver!" I yelled to the man in the front seat.

"I need you to hook that thing back up and take it back where it came from!"

Chip made it clear to me that once he made a deal—fair or not—that thing was ours now.

By that point the cameras had totally disappeared to both of us. We just completely forgot they were there. Chip's arms were flailing around as he circled the boat, tallying up the problems he could find. My arms were flailing as I yelled at him for buying that dumb thing without talking to me first.

When I finally calmed down, I saw how disappointed he was and how bad he felt. I decided to take a deep breath and try to think this thing through.

"Maybe it's not that bad," I said. (I think I was trying to cheer myself up as much as I was trying to console Chip.) "If we fix up the interior and just get it to the point where we can get it onto the water, at least maybe then we can turn around, sell it, and get our money back."

Over the course of the next hour or so, I really started to come around. I took another walk through the boat and started to picture how we could make it livable—maybe even kind of cool. After all, we'd conquered worse. We tore a few things apart right then and there, and I grabbed some paper and sketched out a new layout for the tiny kitchen. I talked to him about potentially finishing an accent wall with shiplap—a kind of rough-textured pine paneling that fans of our show now know all too well.

"*Ship*lap?" Chip laughed. "That seems a little ironic to use on a *ship*, doesn't it?"

"Ha-ha," I replied. I was still not in the mood for his jokes, but this is how Chip backs me off the ledge—with his humor.

Then I asked him to help me lift something on the deck, and he said, "Aye, aye, matey!" in his best pirate voice, and slowly but surely I came around.

I can't believe I'm saying this, but by the end of that afternoon I was actually a little bit excited about taking on such a big challenge. Chip was still deflated that he'd allowed himself to get duped, but he put his arm around me as we started walking back to the truck. I put my head on his shoulder. And the cameras captured the whole thing—just an average, roller-coaster afternoon in the lives of Chip and Joanna Gaines.

The head cameraman came jogging over to us before we drove away. Chip rolled down his window and said sarcastically, "How's *that* for reality TV?" We were both feeling embarrassed that this is how we had spent our last day of trying to get this stinkin' television show.

"Well," the guy said, breaking into a great big smile, "if I do my job, you two just landed yourself a reality TV show."

*What?* We were floored. We couldn't believe it. How was *that* a show? But lo and behold, he was right. That rotten houseboat turned out to be a blessing in disguise. Over the course of the next few months, the production company's head of development, Patrick Jager, championed our show tirelessly—until HGTV decided we were just what they wanted. Apparently one of the big selling points was the "authenticity" we'd shown during that humbling afternoon. We couldn't have scripted it even if we'd tried. There was something about Chip's impulsiveness, his riskiness, combined with my reaction to his riskiness and the way we worked it out as a couple, that landed us the show.

A few months later, the cameras were back—and *Fixer Upper* was born. Our quiet little lives turned completely upside down as our life's work became a hit TV show. After years of toiling away semi-anonymously here in Waco, trying to make ends meet while designing our clients' dream homes and doing our best to raise our four kids right, our world changed in a way that was much different than either of us ever could have imagined.

Now that we've had some time to reflect on it, it's as if our whole lives had been preparing us for this experience. We didn't know it at the time, but it's as if the seeds had been planted long ago.

Have you ever looked at the bud of a magnolia flower? It's a tight little pod that stays closed up for a long time on the end of its branch until one day, out of nowhere, it finally bursts open into this gigantic, gorgeous, fragrant flower that's ten times bigger than the bud itself. It's impossible to imagine that such a big beautiful thing could pop out of that tiny little bud. But it does. And that's sort of what getting "discovered" and sharing our lives on *Fixer Upper* feels like to us.

We never could have imagined being on TV together, touching the lives of so many people, especially back when we were two broke newlyweds sleeping on the floor of our eight-hundred-square-foot house while we renovated it, or when I first opened and then had to *close* my little Magnolia shop on Bosque Boulevard. I have to wonder, though, if it was just a happy coincidence that we decided to name that shop Magnolia. Or was it something more? Because it's staggering to think just how much it has blossomed.

As we finished up writing this book, HGTV was airing the third season of *Fixer Upper,* and we'd started filming seasons four and five. And that's only part of the excitement. Thanks to the show's popularity, we outgrew our beloved "Little Shop on Bosque." In 2015, to make room for all our new customers, we moved the shop into a converted, early twentieth-century cotton-oil mill. Our new property is marked by two giant, rusty, abandoned silos in the heart of downtown Waco—easy to spot from miles away. It's a place where we're proud to welcome our out-of-town visitors.

To get how exciting this is for us, you have to understand where it all started: a little shop, one employee, and a shopgirl who was happy to see eight customers a day. The reality that thousands of visitors are coming to our town to experience Magnolia Market at the Silos is not only an honor, it's one of the single greatest accomplishments of our careers.

We've also had the great thrill of seeing our friends' businesses boom, since we've gotten to incorporate their work and artistry into the shop and the show. That was our goal from the beginning—to bless our community, our friends, and our viewers through this unbelievable platform we've been given.

Chip and I have received generous opportunities to speak all over the country, to give DIY tips on talk shows, to design our own furniture, rug and paint lines, and now to write a book. A book! Can you believe it?

For the two of us, writing these pages has offered a welcome chance to stop and look back on the story of our lives, and it certainly has been an eye-opening process. How many of us take the time to relive half a lifetime's worth of happy memories, cringeworthy failures, and unforgettable adventures together? How many of us get a chance to sit down and talk about the rough times we overcame in the past or to laugh about the stupid mistakes we made when we were young?

Working on this book has allowed us to look back on all the things that brought us here to the farm, to this place we love so much, and to this busy, exciting season in our lives. And let me tell you, it's been one heck of a journey. We're still trying to figure out how to make this new life work for us and our kids, smack-dab in the middle of these exciting new adventures we've been on. Writing it all down has also allowed us to reflect on the inspiration we've picked up and the lessons we've learned along the way—and there have been many!

We feel so blessed to be able to share all of this with you in the hope that you'll find new ways to love the space and season you're in too.

Even after all of this thinking and talking and writing, Chip and I still look at each other at the end of the day and say, "Us? Really?" Honestly, we're still pretty baffled as to why people seem to like watching the two of us be "us" on national TV, because these are the same old things we've been doing since the very day we met. But that's a story for another chapter.

# FIRST DATES AND
# SECOND CHANCES

To this day, I am still not sure what it was about Chip Gaines that made me give him a second chance—because, basically, our first date was over before it even started.

I was working at my father's Firestone automotive shop the day we first met. I'd worked as my dad's office manager through my years at Baylor University and was perfectly happy working there afterward while I tried to figure out what I really wanted to do with my life. The smell of tires, metal, and grease—that place was like a second home to me, and the guys in the shop were all like my big brothers.

On this particular afternoon, they all started teasing me. "You should go out to the lobby, Jo. There's a hot guy out there. Go talk to him!" they said.

"No," I said. "Stop it! I'm not doing that."

I was all of twenty-three, and I wasn't exactly outgoing.

She was a bit awkward—no doubt about that.

I hadn't dated all that much, and I'd never had a serious relationship— nothing that lasted longer than a month or two. I'd always been an introvert and still am (believe it or not). I was also very picky, and I just wasn't the type of girl who struck up conversations with guys I didn't know. I was honestly comfortable being single; I didn't think that much of it.

"Who is this guy, anyway?" I asked, since they all seemed to know him for some reason.

"Oh, they call him Hot John," someone said, laughing.

Hot John? There was no *way* I was going out in that lobby to strike up a conversation with some guy called Hot John. But the guys wouldn't let up, so I finally said, "Fine."

I gathered up a few things from my desk (in case I needed a backup plan) and rounded the corner into the lobby. I quickly realized that Hot John *was* pretty good-looking. He'd obviously just finished a workout—he was dressed head-to-toe in cycling gear and was just standing there, innocently waiting on someone from the back. I tried to think about what I might say to strike up a conversation when I got close enough and quickly settled on the obvious topic: cycling. But just as that thought raced through my head, he looked up from his magazine and smiled right at me.

*Crap,* I thought. I completely lost my nerve. I kept on walking right past him and out the lobby's front door.

When I reached the safety of my dad's outdoor waiting area, I realized just how bad I'd needed the fresh air. I sat on a chair a few down from another customer and immediately started laughing at myself. *Did I really just do that?*

"Hey, what's so funny?" the customer sitting near me asked.

I looked up at him, and before I could even answer he asked, "Wait, aren't you the girl from the commercials?"

"Yeah, that's me," I said, still embarrassed from my awkward encounter with Hot John. I was, in fact, the girl from the commercials. I had some interest in television news. I had even done an internship with CBS in New York City, working under Dan Rather in the news division, and because of that my dad had insisted I go on camera for the local TV ads he ran for his shop.

I was so caught up in my own thoughts that I didn't even get a good look at this guy who had started talking to me. He was wearing a baseball cap and seemed like an average customer. He seemed around my age, maybe a bit older—that was all I really noticed. What did strike me was that he was real chatty, so we wound up sitting there for twenty minutes just shooting the breeze.

Over the course of our conversation, he told me he was a Baylor grad. That struck me as odd. The guys I'd known at Baylor were more the clean-cut type. This guy seemed a little rough-and-tumble, the kind who'd rather work with his hands than keep a corporate calendar. But right off the bat I could tell he was smart—and definitely hardworking. He was just at the shop getting the brakes fixed on his truck. I also found it interesting that he'd stuck around Waco after graduation. "I love this town," he said. "I'm planning to stay in Waco until God makes it clear I'm supposed to move on."

That surprised me too. I loved the way he mentioned God in a way that was so unguarded, and I liked that he wanted to stay in Waco. That was rare for Baylor grads. Normally people shipped themselves straight off to the big cities after graduation.

Speaking of, that whole week I had been debating whether or not to move back to New York City to pursue my dream of broadcast journalism. Most of my friends and family were encouraging me to go, and I was really wrestling with it. It occurred to me this could be my one big chance, but I also really liked it right where I was.

All of a sudden Hot John walked out and said, "Hey, Chip, let's go." I was confused. The man I'd been chatting with—who apparently was named Chip—explained that John was his roommate and that they were business partners. Oh, *of course* these two had come together. I was still completely embarrassed about my initial encounter with Hot John, but I said, "Hi." And then, thankfully, this Chip went right back to our conversation as Hot John took a seat and joined in.

Chip asked me about New York and what I wanted to do, and how long my dad had owned the shop, and what it was I loved about Waco.

He asked about my sisters and my family in general, and what I'd done at Baylor, and if I'd known a few communications majors he'd run around with at school. (I told y'all he was chatty!) Somehow none of these questions seemed intrusive or strange to me at the time, which is funny, because thinking back I find them particularly telling.

At the time, it was just like talking with an old friend.

John finally stood up, and this baseball-cap-wearing customer that John had introduced as Chip followed. "Well, nice talking to you," he said.

"Nice talking to you too," I replied, and that was it. I went back inside. The guys in the shop wanted to know what I thought about Hot John, and I just laughed. "Sorry, guys, I don't think it's gonna work out."

The next day I came back from my lunch break to find a note on my desk: "Chip Gaines called. Call him back." I thought, *Oh, that must be the guy I met yesterday.* So I called him. I honestly thought he was going to ask me about getting a better price on his brakes or something, but instead he said, "Hey, I really enjoyed our conversation yesterday. I was wondering . . . you want to go out sometime?"

And for some reason I said okay—just like that, without any hesitation. It wasn't like me at all. When I hung up the phone, I went, "What in the world just happened!"

So you said okay immediately? I don't even remember that. That's fun! No reservations? Man, I must've been good-lookin'.

What Chip didn't know was I didn't even give myself time to have reservations. Something told me to just go for it.

Cute, Joey. This story makes me love you all over again.

My parents were out of town that week, but I remember calling to tell them, "I'm going on a date with a customer that was in getting his brakes done. I met him yesterday." I guess it's unusual for a twenty-three-year-old to call her parents and tell them she's going on a date, but it was normal for me. I was extremely close to my parents and I was just excited to tell them.

My parents and my little sister, Mary Kay, whom I call Mikey, asked me what this Chip guy looked like, and I said, "I honestly can't tell you. He had a baseball cap on, and the way we were sitting, I didn't really get a good look at him."

When the night of our big date came, I was giddy and a bit anxious. I got ready at my sister's apartment. She and her roommates, Sarah and Katiegh, were all there for moral support, and Chip was supposed to pick me up at six. Six rolls around. No Chip. Then six thirty—still no Chip. I thought, *Well, maybe he thought the date was at seven*, so I gave him the benefit of the doubt. But when seven came and went, I was officially done.

Finally, at seven thirty, a full ninety minutes late, he knocked at the door.

"Don't even answer it," I whispered to my friends. "I don't want to go anywhere with this idiot."

"But we want to see what he looks like!" they said, and so one of them finally opened the door while I hung back out of sight.

"Well, hello, ladies," Chip said as he pushed his way into the apartment. I could tell that he charmed every one of them in about two seconds flat. I finally decided to step out and at least take a look at him. He was not like I remembered at all. This guy had no hair. I'd imagined he had hair under the baseball cap, but nope. Just stubble. And his face was weathered and flushed red, like he'd been working outside in the hot sun all day long. He was wearing a reddish-toned leather jacket, too, and I thought, *Is this red guy even the same guy I was talking to at the shop?*

It turned out that Chip had shaved his head to support a friend of his who was battling cancer.

A bunch of us shaved our heads for a good friend of mine. It was growing back, but it was just about a buzz cut at that point.

I still don't remember what he said that convinced me to walk out the door with him. He didn't even have a plan for our date. He said, "So, Joanna, where do you want to go eat?" He didn't apologize for being late, either. He had so much confidence. I don't know. I can't explain it. Only Chip could be an hour and a half late and have no one mad about it.

I wasn't an hour and a half late. She's making that up. I was, like, twenty minutes late.

Chip was an hour and a half late to *everything*. If I'd known that then, maybe I wouldn't have taken it personally.

Well, I think you're wrong. You're cute, though, and you do have me on the no-plans thing. That was bad. I don't know why I'm like that. I just never have any plans. I like the way things just work themselves out. It's more fun that way. I wasn't nervous about the date or where to eat, and I wasn't nervous about being late.

Out in his truck, Chip asked me again where I'd like to eat, so I suggested a place out in Valley Mills, a small town about thirty minutes from Waco—which, looking back, was a gutsy move for a first date. Thirty minutes was a long time to be in a car if you ran out of things to talk about. But there was a restaurant there in a historic mansion where my parents liked to go. It was really charming, and it was the first place that popped into my head.

The whole drive over there was kind of like a dream. Jo wasn't anything like the girls I typically went out with. But she was so cute, you know? We wound up driving out of town through these back roads—I didn't know where in the heck we were going—and we came up to this mansion with pillars on the front that looked like something you'd see in *Gone with the Wind*.

Everything was going about like I'd expected until we sat down at the table and the owner of the restaurant came over. Everywhere I went in Waco and Dallas, someone was always coming up and talking to me, so I thought maybe this guy was coming over to say hello. Turns out he wasn't coming to talk to me at all. He was coming over to talk to Joanna.

"Hey, sweetheart, how are you? I saw your latest commercial. Tell your mom and dad I said hello, okay?" They talked for quite a while, and my mind started turning, like, *Wow. This girl is a local superstar.*

Dinner was perfect. We were both comfortable with each other for some reason, and the conversation came easy. When the bill came, Chip quickly popped up and took a big roll of cash out of his pocket. I don't think I'd ever seen anyone carry that much cash. My dad was successful, but he kept his money in a bank. Seeing that, I thought, *Oh, that's why he stayed in Waco. He's doing really well for himself!*

You thought I was rich. Ha! What you didn't know is that was probably all the money I had in the world. I always carried cash. I'd carry, like, $1,000 on me in those days. I just loved the way it felt. Plus, I worked with a lot of rough dudes, and some of them expected to be paid in cash.

It's funny because I went to Baylor, where I was surrounded by all these rich kids from rich families, and for whatever reason I was never drawn to that. I was much more comfortable hanging out with the guys who dug ditches. I lived like them, too, whether it was carrying all my money around in my pocket or sitting under some shady tree at lunchtime while they laughed at me trying to eat jalapeños.

After dinner the two of us went and sat on that grand front porch for a while. It was a beautiful night, and I could have just sat there and listened to the silence. But Chip, of course—he had other ideas. I just looked at him until I couldn't even hear him anymore. I remember thinking, *Nope. This guy isn't even close to done.*

In my head, I started to go down the checklist we women put together in our heads and our hearts. I'd always been attracted to people with dark hair. He was blond or redheaded or something in between—it was too short to tell. I would have preferred hair, period.

I'd always been attracted to quiet guys, too, which I knew was a problem because the quiet guys never had the nerve to ask me out, and they certainly never drew me out the way this guy did. Still, he was all over the place. He was talking about the businesses he'd started, and these ideas he had, and how he was buying up little houses and flipping them and renting some out to Baylor students, and I was wondering if he was just a bit crazy.

I liked stability. I liked safety. I liked *traditional* and I liked being on time. And this Chip with the beet-red face wasn't any of those things. I did think he was kind of fascinating, though.

I know this is going to sound strange to some people, but right in the middle of that—right in the middle of me trying to figure this guy out—a little voice in my head said, *That's the man you're going to marry.* I swear to you it was clear as day. It seemed like the voice of God, or maybe it was some deep intuition, but I heard it. In fact, I heard it so loudly that I completely tuned out our conversation and lost focus.

My roommates asked me a million questions after he dropped me off that night: "What was he like? Did he try to kiss you? How was the date?" And my response was that it was good. We had fun. He was a good talker. And no, he didn't try to kiss me. I didn't tell them about that voice in my head. It seemed far too ridiculous. But honestly, if it wasn't for that voice, I'm not sure I would have stuck it out through all the ups and downs of dating a guy like Chip. I was spinning a bit, but I certainly didn't fall instantly head-over-heels for him or anything like that.

It wasn't exactly a love at first sight for me, either. It was a fun date, but I'd been on lots of fun dates. Something was different, though. Joanna impressed me. I couldn't stop thinking about that owner coming up to talk to her. I was honestly the one who normally got the attention. She was totally different from the typical blonde-haired, blue-eyed cheerleader type I tended to date. But the more I thought about her, the more I knew I wanted to see her again.

We made plans to go get coffee the following week, but I had to cancel. I hurt my back. In fact, I needed to go into the hospital for surgery, and I let Chip know that. He seemed real concerned and wished me luck—and then he didn't call me again. He didn't send flowers to the hospital. Nothing.

Flowers to the hospital? After one date?

Yes! That would've been the chivalrous thing to do. Everyone thought it was rude that you didn't call after that.

Huh. Well, I apologize, Jo. I didn't even think about that.

It's okay. I forgive you. I think it turned out okay in the end.

Even though he wasn't what I'd pictured as the type of man I might be interested in, there was just something about Chip Gaines that I couldn't get off my mind. I kept thinking about him—and thinking about just how weird it all was.

Our first date happened at the end of October, and it wasn't until after the turn of the New Year—early January something—that I finally got another phone call from him.

"Hey, Jo, I just wanted to say that I really enjoyed our date, and I think we ought to stop playing all these games," he said.

I was sitting there thinking, *What games is this guy talking about?*

I'd made a bet with Hot John to see who could hold out the longest before calling our dates back. I really wanted that fifty dollars from John! That's the only reason I didn't call.

I think Chip was still dating a few girls off and on then.

Yeah, I think you're right. But I did want to win that fifty dollars, and it was killing me because I kept thinking about you and I really did think you were going to call any day now!

"There's a basketball game tonight. Would you like to go?" Chip asked me. Once again, without hesitation, I said yes, and from that night on, Chip and I started seeing each other almost every day. He would come by the tire shop to visit. He met my parents. I met his parents. I went out and drove around with him to see some of the properties he worked on and to meet some of the guys he worked with in his landscaping business. One guy, Melesio, was like a brother to Chip. I had never seen someone bond so closely to the people he worked with.

After a while, I even offered to help him do some of the books for the little businesses he was running, and he took me up on it. I'd never been around that kind of work before, but I thought it was fun. I thought *he* was fun.

About four months into it, we were shooting hoops in my dad's driveway when Chip stopped in his tracks, held me in his arms, looked into my eyes under the starry sky, and said, "I love you."

And I looked at him and said, "Thank you."

"Thank you?" Chip said.

I know I should have said, "I love you too," but this whole thing had been such a whirlwind, and I was just trying to process it all. No guy had ever told me he loved me before, and here Chip was saying it after what seemed like such a short period of time.

Chip got angry. He grabbed his basketball from under my arm and went storming off with it like a four-year-old.

I really thought, *What in the world is with this girl? I just told her I loved her, and that's all she can say?* It's not like I just went around saying that to people all the time. So saying it was a big deal for me too. But now I was stomping down the driveway going, *Okay, that's it. Am I dating an emotionless cyborg or something? I'm going home.*

Chip took off in his big, white Chevy truck with the Z71 stickers on the side, even squealing his tires a bit as he drove off, and it really sank in what a big deal that must have been for him. I felt bad—so bad that I actually got up the courage to call him later that night. I explained myself, and he said he understood, and by the end of the phone call we were right back to being ourselves.

Two weeks later, when Chip said, "I love you" again, I responded, "I love you too." There was no hesitation. I knew I loved him, and I knew it was okay to say so.

I'm not sure why I ever gave him a second chance when he showed up ninety minutes late for our first date or why I gave him another second chance when he didn't call me for two months after that. And I'm not sure why he gave me a second chance after I blew that romantic moment in the driveway. But I'm very glad I did, and I'm very glad he did too—because sometimes second chances lead to great things.

All of my doubts, all of the things I thought I wanted out of a relationship, and many of the things I thought I wanted out of life itself turned out to be just plain wrong. Instead? That voice from our first date turned out to be the thing that was absolutely right.

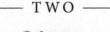

# NEW DIRECTIONS

The first year Chip and I dated turned out to be my year of letting go—letting go of the notion that my life was going to be predictable in any way, shape, or form.

By his midtwenties, Chip had already been through a whole series of different businesses. Every time I thought I'd heard it all, he would tell me about something else that he'd done to earn a buck.

Like in college, I sold Scantron test forms. Those are the answer cards you use when taking certain kinds of tests. The teachers were able to run them through machines, and that sped up the grading process. Students at Baylor had to buy and bring their own Scantron forms to class with them, but hardly anyone ever remembered to do it. So before a test, the teacher would sit up at the front and say, "Who didn't bring their Scantron?" Two-thirds of the class would raise their hands, and she would sell them Scantron forms for two dollars apiece. This was kind of a slap on the wrist, so-to-speak, because at the bookstore they only cost, like, a dime each.

I went to the bookstore and bought a whole bunch of these things, and the next time she offered to sell some, I stood up and said, "Mine are only a dollar." I had so many people buy a Scantron that day, I walked away feeling pretty good about it. After all, I was a business major. I thought that move should've earned me an instant A.

I also sold books for a company called Southwestern Book Company for two summers in college. It was a program where you were sent to a town, usually pretty far from home. Your first objective was to convince people you'd never met to put you up for the summer—for free! And then you'd walk around town selling books door-to-door.

I'll tell you—that job changed my perspective as a college student. If you sold a lot of books you could pocket a lot of money, and because of the setup, you had really low overhead. The downside was that it was a ton of work, and it was far from home. Most kids weren't willing to do that.

I only spent about three dollars a day on a sandwich and some eggs, so all of the money I made went into my pocket. If I'd been a lifeguard or if I had waited tables over the summers, I would have wound up going out with my buddies and spending half my pay jacking around. But doing that program was almost like being sent to an island somewhere where all you do is work and sleep. And I was good at it.

I remember reading about work on Alaskan fishing boats where, if things worked out, you could earn north of $6,000 a month. It was grueling, potentially deadly stuff, but with no overhead, the money was all yours. These were the kinds of things I'd sit and think about while I was in class. I realized most people don't want to do what it takes to do a lot of things. I made up my mind right then and there—I would do whatever it takes to be successful.

The second summer, in the middle of selling books, I went to east Texas to open a fireworks stand. You can only sell fireworks in Texas during the two weeks before the Fourth of July, so I took the money I'd earned from half a summer's worth of bookselling and bought a fireworks stand and inventory. This probably seemed like a bonehead move to my parents, but I'd heard there was good money in it.

My friend Eric and I went in on the stand together. And it was not easy—no doubt about that—but I learned a lot. It was my first experience with investing. I did that the next two summers as well, opening three or four stands in east Texas, and my friend's uncle, whom I call Uncle Ricky, played a huge role in all of that. From selling books I knew I enjoyed hard work and the thrill of selling, but it was Uncle Ricky who recognized the entrepreneur in me and encouraged me to follow that dream.

There was something about the way Ricky would say, "Chip, you can do this," that made me believe I could. He really believed in me and trained me to some extent about simple business practices like paying taxes or understanding assets versus liabilities.

I took all that experience and used it to open up a lawn-mowing business, which quickly expanded into a full landscaping business with employees, equipment, and clients. Then I got the idea to buy some cheap properties on Third Street in Waco—sort of on the other side of the tracks, so to speak, but within a mile or so of the Baylor campus—so I could rent them out to incoming college students.

I was rocking and rolling. I wasn't inventing Facebook or anything like that, but I was definitely what you would call a serial entrepreneur.

Chip's experimentation with lots of different kinds of businesses had eventually evolved into flipping houses. By the time we met, he'd successfully done it for a few years. Flipping seemed to be his thing. I have to say it quickly became my favorite venture of his too.

When explaining to my friends and family what Chip did, I was always a little at a loss. He wasn't a realtor—at least people would've been able to understand that—and I'd never known a career could be made out of buying and selling houses. So even though I spent a lot of my time with Chip kind of playing catch-up to understand it all, it was exciting to me.

As I said before, Chip was a smart guy. Unconventional, maybe, but he always had the entrepreneurial spirit and business sense to back it up. I was intrigued by this lifestyle of his, maybe because it was wildly different from the "safe" world I'd grown up in. Every day seemed to bring a new adventure, because Chip really did refuse to be put in the nine-to-five box people filed themselves into after college graduation.

Even when things got complicated, Chip remained fearless. It seemed as if nothing could stop him, and I was hooked. I think that's why, when we were first dating in our twenties, we were doing things most people our age weren't doing.

Before he ever graduated from college, Chip had already figured out the game—banking, negotiations, selling, all of it. Most people in college are studying and dating, and Chip was certainly doing his fair share of that. But mostly he spent his time thinking, *What's the next business I can get into?* In that regard, he was kind of a step ahead of a lot of our peers.

By the time I started helping him with his properties, Chip was known as the unofficial "Mayor of Third Street." He owned a bunch of tiny little houses along this stretch of road that was also home to a school for troubled youth. Before he came in and fixed up some of the old houses to rent to Baylor students, a lot of people in Waco just steered clear of Third Street. But Chip was his fearless self and saw the area as a spot full of underpriced properties with potential.

The kids at the school were young, and there was something about that age group that made Chip think he still had time to make a difference. He would cruise up and down that street on his four-wheeler, checking on the progress at his various properties and checking in to make sure the tenants didn't need anything, and when he saw those kids walking by after school, he'd get into conversations and joke around with them.

He wound up convincing a few of those kids to help out doing lawns and odd jobs on the properties he owned, and he paid them well, which ended up making him a pretty popular guy with them. It seemed that every time he'd give one a job, four more would show up the next day, ready to earn a little money. It was inspiring to watch him work and to see how well he got along with everyone from his crew to his clients to those kids to Uncle Ricky, whom he introduced me to early on.

An interesting side note: Ricky and his wife made a hobby of importing antiques from Europe. They turned their little backyard into an absolute oasis full of old metal and wooden architectural pieces that he built into the landscape, and every time we went over there the backyard had some new feature added to it. It was like walking from an ordinary Texas front porch into an exotic vacation every time you walked out the back door. I remember thinking, even back then, *I would love to do something like that someday.*

So when Chip asked me to help him out that first summer we were dating, as he repainted and generally got his properties fixed up before the new Baylor students arrived in the fall, I was happy to do it. I didn't know anything about interior design or construction—I'd been a communications major, for heaven's sake—but I was more than content being his gofer.

To be honest, I didn't know any more about interior design or construction than Jo did. I learned it all on the fly. If I needed to put a fence in—or anything else, for that matter—I would just get my hands dirty and figure it out. Everything I did was that way. Story of my life!

I was still working at my dad's shop, too, but it was fun for me to see Chip's collection of little houses get all cleaned up. I liked thinking about the students who would soon be living in them and remembering what it had felt like to move into my first apartment. I wanted to make sure everything was right for those kids.

Most of the houses weren't much bigger than eight hundred square feet, so there wasn't a lot to work with, but I quickly saw how new carpet or a fresh paint color could change the whole atmosphere in a house that small. I liked the feeling of getting these jobs done and then watching the way those kids and their parents would go nuts as they were moving in.

There was something rewarding about that kind of work. Even if it was something as simple as painting one room, each project had a beginning, middle, and end. You could stand back and actually see what you'd accomplished at the end of the day, and there was something very satisfying in that for me—on top of how much fun it was just to watch Chip do his thing and try to imagine what he might do next.

It was more than just business. With Chip, it was everything. He was wild at heart, really. If you tried to give him a rule, he would break it. If you gave Chip a boundary, he would cross it.

Chip was just Chip. There was no box for this guy.

There's this movie, *Legends of the Fall,* where the character named Tristan goes off into these wild places. I've always thought of myself as kind of like that.

And (case in point) the things that would come out of his mouth were unlike anything anyone else would ever think to say. Sometimes it would take me a second to figure out whether he was joking around or drop-dead serious. He kept me on my toes—and I liked it.

Chip was also extremely kind and giving. I swear every time we'd see a homeless guy, Chip would stop and talk to him. Sometimes he'd give him money. Sometimes he'd give him a job for the day. Heck, if the weather was bad, he'd even put him up in a hotel.

We'd be walking downtown, and I'd hear, "Chip. Hey, Chip!" and I'd turn to see a person approaching us who, frankly, might have scared me if I was walking downtown by myself. Chip wouldn't be scared. He'd know the guy by name: "James! How's it going, brother?" It seemed as if every homeless guy in Waco knew Chip Gaines.

On the flip side, every banker in Waco knew Chip too. And he talked to those two very different groups of people exactly the same way. There was never any difference in Chip's demeanor. His enthusiasm for life and work and people was just infectious, and he surprised me with it again and again. At least once a day I caught myself thinking, *Wow, this guy!*

Best of all, as happy as Chip Gaines was, he seemed happiest around me.

I'm a generally happy person. My mom says I was a happy baby. But it's a fact—I was always happiest around Jo. And I still am.

One pretty amazing thing we learned early on was that the more time we spent together, the better our relationship was. I think a lot of couples feel the need to get away from each other now and then, to take little breaks, and they come back after a girls' weekend or a guys' fishing trip or something all refreshed and happy to reconnect because they missed each other.

We were just the opposite, and still are. We seem to give each other energy. We function better together than we do apart, and I don't think either one of us has ever felt the urge to say, "I need a break from you."

Don't get me wrong; we've certainly had our share of disappointment and arguments, but we just always wanted to tackle our issues together.

The two of us never talked about marriage during that first year we were together, but I knew pretty quickly that we were in this for the long haul, and I almost had to convince myself that it was okay to be in love with this man. I kept reminding myself, "With Chip, my life isn't gonna look like what I thought it was gonna look like—but there *will* be adventure, and there *will* be some fun."

My parents were the type of people who locked their doors and had an alarm system. For my whole life they encouraged me to go after what

I wanted, to get a good education, even to go to New York for that internship. But they also encouraged me to use caution—and I did.

Chip was the polar opposite. For example, whenever we went out shopping or to restaurants, he would leave his keys in the car. Who leaves their keys in the car in today's world? It was a real problem for us for a while, because my first instinct when I got out of the car was to lock the doors. So we'd come back after dinner and realize I'd locked Chip's keys in the car again.

I remember that! In college, I would not only leave my keys in the car, but half the time I would forget and leave it running.

What's ironic about Jo and my parents is Jo's parents were pretty much hippies in their younger years. Her dad served in Vietnam, and he was this tall, quiet, lanky guy with glasses, and her mom was this vivacious Korean woman who just loved life. They both have the best stories. When I first saw pictures of the two of them from before Jo was born, they looked like John Lennon and Yoko Ono. They were right in the thick of all that went on during the sixties. But despite that youthful "rebellion," they turned out to be the kind of cautious parents who were concerned with traditions and playing it safe.

My parents both grew up in a little bitty town called Archer City, Texas, and they were straight as an arrow, but they left the garage door open all day, even when they were out. They wouldn't even think about locking the doors. My mom saw an upside to everything, and I think that's part of what made me so optimistic and adventurous.

I have to say, I'm very thankful that Jo's parents were all right with us being together. They could have said, "This guy is not gonna work, and you need to move in a different direction." And honestly, Jo was so obedient that, just for the sake of responsibility or obligation or whatever you want to call it, she might have broken it off. But her parents, even early on, were supportive and encouraging. And my parents were of course supportive of her. They still say to this day she is the best thing that ever happened to me.

Despite all the differences between my dad and Chip, Dad knew that he had a good heart, and he saw something in Chip that he knew was right for me.

People say opposites attract, and I think the fact that Chip and I were together for anything beyond a first date proves that point pretty well. But the fact that we *stayed* together goes to something a little deeper. The fact that we were opposites on the surface didn't negate the fact that we were both raised by loving parents, in loving families, and that we both love our families dearly. Our roots were important to both of us, and that one common bond, to me, plays a big role in what has kept us together.

Not that we're perfect or anything. Don't get the wrong idea. There were times when we would fight like cats and dogs. And Jo's tough. But there was just something about her. We'd work through it. Whatever stupid mistake I made—and there was plenty of stuff that set her off—we'd find a way to get through it, and we'd wind up being even closer to each other in the end. Every time.

Jo was more perfect for me than I ever could have imagined. After we'd been dating about a year, I honestly couldn't imagine my life without her. So I decided to do the traditional thing and went and asked Jo's dad for her hand in marriage. Honestly, that was one of the best days of my life. I couldn't have been more nervous, and he was just so supportive. Both of our families were supportive. And as soon as I was over that hurdle, I started planning a way to surprise her and ask her to marry me in a way that she'd never forget.

Chip told me he'd been invited to a private concert, and he asked me if I wanted to go. He was vague about what kind of music it was or what this concert was all about, but I didn't care. I pretty much wanted to go anywhere Chip wanted to take me.

"Okay, great!" he said. "Well, you've got to get really dressed up, and it's in Archer City."

I knew that both of Chip's parents had gone to high school in that sweet little town, which was the setting for Larry McMurtry's famous novel, *The Last Picture Show,* and the movie of the same name starring Cybill Shepherd and Jeff Bridges. The old theater that inspired the book and film was still there, and I knew they had concerts in that venue from time to time, so nothing seemed unusual about Chip's request, even though we would have to drive four hours to get there. I honestly didn't suspect a thing. I was just excited.

We wound up rolling into Archer City at about seven o'clock that night. But instead of pulling up near the theater, Chip pulled into this little shopping center and drove us around to a door in the back.

"Chip, where are you taking me?" I asked.

"Just come on," he said. He was all smiles.

I was thinking, *Well, this must be a super private concert.* He took me into this unmarked hallway, and at first he seemed kind of lost, as if he was trying to figure out where he was going. Then all of a sudden Chip fell down to one knee and sort of wobbled to one side. I thought he was having a heart attack or something.

"Chip? Are you okay?" I said.

I was wearing a peacoat—it was cold out—and when I knelt down, my knee pinned the bottom of my coat to the ground so I couldn't sit back up straight. I had to put my hand against the wall so I could lean and get the jacket out from under me.

Then he looked at me. I realized he was down on one knee on purpose. He got real calm, and he took my hand, and he said, "I want to spend the rest of my life with you." I was in total shock—even more so than I was on my dad's driveway basketball court when Chip first said, "I love you."

"Oh my goodness!" was the only thing I could get out. I was so taken aback, and so happy, but *so* confused.

"Chip," I said, kind of giggling and giddy at the whole thing. "Babe, why are we doing this in a hallway?"

Chip got a funny smile on his face, a smile I'd never seen before, and he said, "Well, knock on the door." We were standing beside an unmarked door in that unmarked hallway, and I could not figure out for the life of me what he was up to. I shook my head and went ahead and knocked—and the door opened.

Behind it stood a man who looked like Geppetto from *Pinocchio*, wearing a leather apron and a magnifying visor on his head.

"Welcome to my jewelry shop," the man said. "You're here to design your ring."

I just about melted. The shopping center was closed, so we had the whole store to ourselves. The jeweler was a man named Billy Holder, who had gone to high school with Chip's dad, and they'd worked this whole thing out in advance. The fact that the selection of the ring tied back to Chip's roots and family history made it all the more special for me.

I couldn't get over the fact that Chip had arranged all of this just for me. *When did he have the time? How did he keep it all a secret?* I wondered. I basically got the chance to sit and sift through Billy's entire inventory of diamonds and settings and pick my engagement ring right there on the spot.

I gave her the pick of any eighty-dollar diamond she wanted.

He's kidding. His budget was actually quite a bit more than eighty dollars. We joked about that, though, because my dad had only had eighty dollars to spend on my mom's engagement ring, and she'd loved it anyway. As soon as they could afford it, she upgraded. But I was so happy, I think I would have been happy with an eighty-dollar ring if that was all Chip could afford.

Sure, if you were the one to pick it out! Even back then, I was smart enough to know you were real opinionated. If I'd gone and picked out the ring myself, I could literally have seen you going, "Hey, I really do love you, and you and me are gonna work out fine, but there's no way that's the ring I'm gonna wear."

Oh, and just to clarify about my answer to Chip—at some point after saying, "Oh my goodness," I did say yes.

Chip said his mom had loaned him some money, so I was able to get something really special. We didn't have tens of thousands of dollars to spend, and thankfully we weren't buying diamonds in Beverly Hills. I was able to pick out a nice round diamond and a beautiful, antique-looking platinum setting.

I had a blast sitting there with Billy, designing the perfect ring. Chip just sat there, patiently observing every second of it. After we finished designing, Billy said he would need some time to work on the ring, so he gave me a substitute to wear for the time being, just for fun. It was a great big, gaudy fake diamond that he'd put together so I would have something to show off to my friends and family.

"Your parents are gonna go crazy wondering how much money you spent on this!" Billy said to Chip with a laugh.

There was no private concert that night, but Chip did have more in store for me. From Billy's shop we drove over to this cute little Archer City hotel for dinner. My parents, my little sister, Chip's parents, and his sister were all there waiting to celebrate our engagement with us.

There were all sorts of hugs and tears of joy that made that night the most perfect night ever, and of course they were all taken aback by the size of my "diamond." It's funny to me that, even way back then, they all seemed to realize that a flashy ring just wasn't my style. They expected to see me wearing something a little subtler, a little smaller, a little more classic maybe. But we strung them along for a good long while, and we all had a good laugh when Chip finally revealed that the ring was fake.

Twelve years later, we had the opportunity to invite Billy Holder out to the farm for our anniversary party. Chip surprised me that night with a twelve-year anniversary strand of pearls that Billy hand-delivered to me, and we had the cameras there to capture the whole moment. It aired as part of our third season. But what the cameras didn't show was the moment when we went back to the farm and found Billy sitting on my front porch holding a selection of diamonds on a black velvet tray. "Chip wants you to upgrade," he said to me.

"My engagement ring?" I said.

"Yes! He knows you love the setting, but he wants you to be able to pick out a better diamond like your mom did."

That first diamond was beautiful, but it was simple in nature. It was all we could afford back then, but at this point I wanted to do something nicer. Something bigger. So I'd told Billy to bring some options so we could replace it with something else. I thought of it as an investment of sorts, and I wanted it to be perfect.

So Billy showed me all of these beautiful diamonds and told me I could have my pick. That's supposed to be every girl's dream, right? But I looked him in the eye, and I said, "I'm sorry, but no. This is the original diamond I picked, and it's perfect just the way it is."

It wasn't a "perfect" diamond, but it was perfect for me. I felt bad that Billy wasn't going to make the big sale he was hoping for that day, but I don't ever want to replace that diamond *or* that ring. To me, my ring is part of our story.

If I looked down at my hand and saw a more expensive diamond in that setting, it somehow wouldn't fit. I would know that we couldn't have afforded that diamond back when we first got engaged. The story wouldn't add up.

But this ring, with this diamond, the one I wear every day—this ring *fits*. When I look at it, I remember picking out that very diamond on the night of our engagement and looking at it through the little magnifier. I think about the look on Chip's face when he looked up at me in that hallway. And inevitably, I can't stop myself from thinking of where it led us six months later: our wedding.

# THREE

# SOMETHING OLD, SOMETHING NEW

Sometimes I think, *If I were to do my wedding today, I would do things differently.* With everything I've learned, the places I've gone, the design ideas I've seen, I would want to include all sorts of details that I never could have even imagined back then.

But then I flip open our wedding album and see the smiling faces of the people we love all gathered in that place where we chose to celebrate our special day together, and just as with my engagement ring, any desire for something different or fancier melts away. Our wedding was perfect just the way it was. Everything we cared about was exactly the way we wanted. When I look back, I realize I wouldn't change a single thing.

Chip and I got married here in Waco on May 31, 2003, at the Earle Harrison House, a historic mansion that looks an awful lot like the place where we had our first date—a stately manor with grand pillars and a gorgeous garden. We actually chose the location primarily because of its parklike setting. We wanted an outdoor wedding, and the gardens there were filled with roses.

The place was completely covered in flowers climbing high on grand arbors that our guests would walk under. The setting was so beautiful just the way it was. I didn't need much of a budget for flowers. I loved magnolias even back then, before the shop came along, so we cut individual magnolia leaves for our guests to use as fans.

My parents had sat us down shortly after we announced our engagement and made us an offer. They'd been married on the steps of a courthouse, and with that in mind they'd said they were going to give us a certain amount of money as an up-front wedding gift. We could use that money for whatever we wanted—to throw a nicer wedding than we could afford on our own (although *anything* would have been more than we could afford on our own at that point) or to throw a simple wedding and use that money on a down payment for a home or a honeymoon or whatever we chose.

Chip and I decided that we would use the money for the wedding. Since our plan was to move into one of his soon-to-be-vacated student rental houses on Third Street for the summer, we didn't need extra for a down payment. And Chip's parents had been kind enough to take care of the honeymoon, so we were set.

I had no desire for a high-priced designer dress, so I went out shopping with my mom and found one off the rack for around five hundred dollars. Just a simple, white, Cinderella-looking dress with a lace-up back—narrow at the waist and then flowing out through the skirt. Chip and his groomsmen wore rented tuxedos from the mall. We weren't interested in capturing the latest trends or trying to impress anybody. We just wanted it to be beautiful, and the best way I knew to do that was to stick to a classic, timeless look, so black-and-white attire with red roses was the palette we chose. Plus, we knew all of those beautiful white roses in the Harrison House gardens would give us the perfect backdrop we dreamed of.

The day before the wedding, we went over to the property for the rehearsal and I just about died: the estate had pruned all of the roses. They were gone—every last one of them! There was nothing there but empty stems. The arbors, the arch over the altar, everything was just leaves and thorns.

Sadly, it just happened to be the time of year to prune the roses. It was a professionally kept garden, like an arboretum, and the time had come. I mean, I *think* they could have waited an extra day or two know-ing they had a wedding that weekend, but it was too late to argue. In a last-minute attempt to save the scene, we scrambled to our parents to ask for a flower budget. We bought hundreds and hundreds of white roses and stuck them in bunches all over the arbors and barren bushes, doing our best to fill in a million holes and make it look like the real roses were still there.

When I look at pictures now, it may be obvious that those roses had been stuck in by hand, but that wasn't the point. It was honestly almost *better* that all of our closest friends and family had come together at the last minute and tried to turn this venue back into the place we'd been dreaming about.

It really was perfect—perfect for *us*—and part of the reason for that is we broke tradition in some ways. For example, Chip insisted that his dog, Shiner, be in the wedding. We haven't mentioned Chip's dog yet, but that mutt was Chip's best friend. I still swear to this day that he loved that dog more than he loved me. My bridesmaids weren't crazy about the idea of Shiner being a member of the wedding party, but Chip wouldn't budge. Heck, Shiner would've been Chip's best man if he could've stood at the end of that aisle and held those rings. But we compromised and set him up under a gorgeous oak tree so he could be comfortable in the shade as he watched his old man get married.

My dad and I arrived at the ceremony by horse-drawn carriage. A trumpeter played us in. We had a little string quartet and a beautiful couple who sang during the ceremony. All of our closest friends were there. It was a day we'll never forget.

I still look back at it as one of the best days of my life. A lot of my friends and her friends met for the first time at this wedding, because we were literally from different universes. But they were all so impor-tant to us, and I just remember that all my buddies were like, "She has got the sweetest friends!"

All these people kind of came together and became buddies. It was great. And there were some funny coincidences too. Jo had twins in her wedding party, and I had twins in mine. I mean, what are the chances of that?

Chip's dad was his best man. My sisters were my maid and matron of honor. The fact that our friends got along so well and that we both put family first were just more signs to me that Chip and I weren't all that different where it counted. There were a lot of similarities between us, and that day seemed to be filled with affirmations of just how much we truly belonged together.

The wedding seemed to have a ripple effect too. My sister Mary Kay brought this guy to the wedding that she'd only been on a few dates with. His name was David. Well, she caught the bouquet, he caught the garter, and they wound up getting married too. How's that for a story?

⁕

Chip and I started our honeymoon off in New York City, where I had done my internship. One of my favorite things to do when I lived alone in New York was just walk its streets. There are fascinating landmarks around every corner, people of every culture and background and style you could ever imagine, and so many interesting shops and restaurants. No matter how many times you walked those streets, you would always, always find something new.

One of the most surprising finds to me were the little individual shops and boutiques, whether they were clothing stores or home furnishing stores or gift shops. It was almost as if the owners of those little individual shops had to work extra hard to make sure their businesses could compete with the big chains and expensive stores all over town—and the results were incredible.

There always seemed to be a candle burning, filling those shops with the delicious scents. It wasn't unusual to see fresh flowers on the counter next to the cash register or for the shopkeeper to offer you a cup of coffee or tea while you browsed. There was something just wonderfully inviting and warm about those places that made me feel very connected in a city that could sometimes feel big and overwhelming.

I loved taking Chip to that great big city and showing him a side of me he hadn't seen before. We acted like rich kids and stayed in a suite at the Drake Hotel, a high-end, first-class place on Park Avenue that had once played host to celebrities like Frank Sinatra and Lillian Gish. But that was just the starting point for our adventure.

We set aside a full two weeks for our honeymoon, and other than those couple of nights at the Drake, we made no plans whatsoever. We decided to rent a little car and just go wherever the day took us. We headed upstate and marveled as the massive city gave way so quickly to hills and rivers and fields full of flowers. Before long the tallest buildings around were the silos on old-fashioned farms that dotted the landscape.

Chip and I both had an affection for farms and old barns and silos, and we decided it would be fun to go explore. If we saw an abandoned barn, all gray and weathered and tipping over in some empty field, we'd stop and go walk around it, even duck inside just to see what was there. Occasionally we'd find old bottles and farm equipment, and I always wondered why someone had just up and abandoned them there for all those years.

The thing I found interesting was just how beautiful everything looked. The rust, the age, the weathering—maybe it was just because we were in love, but everything we saw in those old abandoned barns, both inside and out, seemed to capture and reflect the beauty of the land and the air and the early summer scents in that beautiful corner of the world. Even the dust in those old barns seemed to rise up on purpose, helping to illuminate those old forgotten spaces with streams of sunlight that crept through the cracks in the wood.

We didn't have Google Maps in 2003, so we spent that honeymoon road trip following our intuition and heeding the attraction of little signs on the side of the road: "Antiques" or "Bed & Breakfast" or "Pick-Ur-Own!" We agreed that we would drive until we were both dead tired and then find someplace to lay our heads wherever we happened to wind up.

On the first night we ran into this place called the Mohonk Mountain House. We'd been driving along the cliffs of the Hudson River, and then all of a sudden this hotel made of stone rose up in front of our eyes. It looked just like some sort of medieval castle.

It was late, and we were exhausted from all of our exploring, and we both thought we'd died or something. "Is this place for real? Or did we just drive off that cliff to get here?" It was so weird just to cruise into some driveway and have no idea what to expect and then find a place like that.

We wandered into the lobby half expecting it to be our final resting place.

The good news is we weren't dead, and when we told the nice people at the front desk that we were on our honeymoon, they put us up in a gorgeous penthouse suite for the price of a regular room.

People wound up giving us deals like that almost everywhere we went on that trip. It was incredible. And thank goodness, because we were already low on funds.

From there, we decided to continue up into New England, meandering across the Berkshires in western Massachusetts, cutting through the country roads of southern New Hampshire, and heading north to explore as much of the crashing Atlantic on the rocky Maine coast as we could. We stayed off the interstates and took back roads as much as possible, stopping at antiques stores and mom-and-pop shops and cute old barns and farmhouses—whatever caught our eye. One night we stayed in the dreamiest bed-and-breakfast right on a farm, where we ate fresh eggs and a home-cooked meal in the morning. Both of us agreed, "What could be better than that?"

Before I met Chip, I was basically a city girl—or maybe a suburban girl. As a kid I lived in a typical cookie-cutter neighborhood in Wichita, Kansas. We lived there until I was twelve, while my dad kind of worked his way up the corporate ladder for Firestone. But as a small child I would often go visit my friend's farm. She had silos that we would play in—I thought that was the coolest thing.

My friend hated living out on that farm. She wanted to come play at my house so she could be in a neighborhood, riding bikes with all my friends. But I liked going to her house because it *was* a farm. We would pretend we were these farm girls that wore aprons, and we'd come up with stories like, "Let's pretend that Bobby got stuck in the silo." We played so much make-believe at that farm that I feel as though farm living was a part of my past, even though it really wasn't. Driving through the beautiful farmlands along the back roads of New York brought back the memories of my time spent there.

The grass is always greener, right? We were both brought up in these sort of cookie-cutter neighborhoods, but in my case, I loved going to my granddad's ranch. That was definitely where I got the cowboy in my personality. My granddad J. B. was a bona fide cowboy. He was like the Marlboro man, literally—smoked cigarettes, tall, lean, great-looking dude, always had this gorgeous cowboy hat on, wore long-sleeved shirts and long pants every day of his life, even when it was a hundred degrees outside. He was just one of these iconic characters. I still to this day think of him as the hero of all heroes, the legend of all legends.

I don't mean to overstate that, because my dad was a huge hero to me too. He was the one who was there, who loved us, who was at every ball game, and my granddad wasn't the doting, overtly loving kind of guy. But he was kind of the patriarch of the family, and spending time with him on that ranch made a big impact on my life.

I may have grown up in the suburbs, like most kids did, but I've always felt like J. B. and I had a lot in common. And I've always felt like I was born a hundred years too late.

For either of us to romanticize farm life was probably a silly thing to do. It's a lot of work. For my friend, living on a farm just meant she had a whole lot of chores to do. But no matter how much I heard her complain, I still thought, *That's what I want someday.* So having that little taste of farm life on our honeymoon sure felt right to both of us.

Days later, somewhere along the woodsy coast of Maine, at around eleven o'clock at night, we had another memorable moment. We were tooling around a corner when Chip slammed on the brakes, squealing to a dead stop. He and I both stared out through the windshield and said, "What in the world is that?!"

Luckily we weren't in a hurry and weren't driving too fast, because right in front of us was this big, awkward-looking moose standing right in the middle of the road. Neither one of us had ever seen one in person, and we just could not believe how big this thing was. It was like a dream come true for me to come across an animal like that in the wild.

Once I realized what it was, I was like, "What should we do? I feel like we should do something!" But Jo said, "Let the poor thing go," so I did. We watched that majestic beast wander off into the woods and disappear in the darkness just as fast as he'd shown up in our headlights.

I feel like the moose was our final big find of that trip. We were both tired, and after seeing something that magnificent, we decided it was time to head home. We took a different route down through Boston and realized as we drove through the city that we were basically out of money.

We had nothing left. We stayed on the interstates after that and made it back to New York with as few stops as possible, arriving just in time to fly back home.

Jo's idea of being "broke" was when she had, like, $1,000 left in the bank. But "broke" for me meant actually broke. I wasn't much for bank accounts or credit cards back then. So once we got back to Waco, we literally had no money left for a hotel room or anything. We had no choice but to go straight to the vacated rental house we were planning to move into.

The students had just moved out of it while we were on our honeymoon, and it was nighttime when we got back home, so we didn't have a chance to get in and inspect it or clean the place or anything like that. We just drove in from the airport and pulled up in front of that little yellow house on Third Street, at the end of this dreamy honeymoon of a lifetime—

And Chip carried me over the threshold. Right into a nightmare.

# FOUR

# THE HONEYMOON'S OVER

The rental houses on Third Street that Chip owned when we got married were really small, and not the most attractive homes. I wouldn't have chosen to live in any one of them if I could avoid it. Thankfully, though, the nicest one of the bunch happened to open up at the end of the spring semester, and Chip hadn't put any summer renters into it yet. It was a yellow ranch-style with a nice white porch on the front and a pair of huge magnolia trees in the yard, and it was bigger than the rest—maybe twelve hundred square feet or so. It was just pretty enough that I was excited to live there and fix it up—to make it feel like our very own home.

Chip and I were both exhausted when we finally pulled up in front of that house, but we were still riding the glow of our honeymoon, and I was so excited as he carried me over the threshold—until the smell nearly knocked us over.

"Oh my word," I said, pinching my nose and trying to hold my breath so I wouldn't gag. "What is that?"

Chip flicked the light switch, and the light didn't come on. He flicked it up and down a few times, then felt his way forward in the darkness and tried another switch.

"The electricity's off," he said. "The girls must've had it shut off when they moved out."

"Didn't you transfer it back into your name?" I asked.

"I guess not. I'm sorry, babe," Chip said.

"Chip, *what* is that *smell*?"

It was the middle of June in Waco, Texas. The temperature had been up over a hundred degrees for days on end, and the humidity was stifling, amplifying whatever that rotten smell was coming from the kitchen. Chip always carries a knife and a flashlight, and it sure came in handy that night. Chip made his way back there and found that the fridge still had a bunch of food left in it, including a bunch of ground beef that had just sat there rotting since whenever the electricity went out.

The food was literally just smoldering in this hundred-degree house. So we went from living in a swanky hotel room on Park Avenue in New York City to this disgusting, humid stink of a place that felt more like the site of a crime scene than a home at this point. Honestly, I hadn't thought it through very well. But it was late, and we were tired, and I just focused on making the most of this awful situation.

So we opened some windows and brought our bags in, and I told Jo we'd just tough it out and sleep on the floor and clean it all up in the morning. That's when she started crying.

I lay down on the floor thinking, *Is this what my life is going to look like now that I married Chip? Is this my new normal?*

That's when another smell hit me. It was in the carpet.

"Chip, did those girls have a dog here?" I asked.

"They had a couple of dogs," he answered. "Why?"

You could smell it. In the carpet. It was nasty. I was just lying there with my head next to some old dog urine stain that had been heated by the Texas summer heat.

It was like microwaved dog pee.

It was. It was awful. It was three in the morning. And I finally said, "Chip, I'm not sleeping in this house."

We were broke. We couldn't go to a hotel. There was no way we were gonna go knock on one of our parents' doors at that time of night.

That's when I got an idea. We happened to have Chip's parents' old RV parked in a vacant lot a few blocks down. We had some of our things in there and had been using it basically as a storage unit until we moved in. "Let's get in the RV. We'll go find somewhere to plug it in, and we'll have AC," I said.

As we stepped outside, the skies opened up. It started pouring rain. When we finally got into the RV, soaking wet, we pulled down the road a ways and Chip said, "I know where we can go." It was raining so hard we could barely see through the windshield, and all of a sudden Chip turned the RV into a cemetery.

"Why are you pulling in to a cemetery?" I asked him.

"We're not going to the cemetery," Chip said. "It's just *next to* a cemetery. There's an RV park back here."

"Are you kidding me? Could this get any worse?"

"Oh, quit it. You're going to love it once I get this AC fired up."

Chip decided to go flying through the median between two rows of RV parking, not realizing it was set up like a culvert for drainage and rain runoff. That RV bounced so hard that, had it not been for our seat belts, we would've both been catapulted through the roof of that vehicle.

"What was that?!"

"I don't know," Chip said.

I tried to put it in reverse, and then forward, and then reverse again, and the thing just wouldn't move. I hopped out to take a look and couldn't believe it. There was a movie a few years ago where the main character gets his RV caught on this fulcrum and it's sitting there teetering with both sets of wheels up in the air. Well, we sort of did the opposite. We went across this valley, and because the RV was so long, the butt end of it got stuck on the little hill behind us, and the front end got stuck on the little hill in front of us, and the wheels were just sort of hanging there in between. I crawled back into the RV soaking wet and gave Jo the bad news.

We had no place to go, no place to plug in so we could run the AC; it was pouring rain so we couldn't really walk anywhere to get help. And at that point I was just done. We wound up toughing it out and spending the first night after our honeymoon in a hot, old RV packed full of our belongings, suspended between two bumps in the road.

The next morning, someone from the RV park spotted us and was kind enough to call a tow truck. The first truck they sent wasn't big enough, so they had to call in a semi tow truck. One of the big ones. We were freaking out, of course, 'cause we were flat broke. (Are you starting to pick up on a theme here? We stayed flat broke a lot of the time early on.) We didn't know how we were going to pay this guy. But then our very last little honeymooner's miracle came through. That truck driver said, "Well, guys, it looks like the honeymoon is over. This one's on us."

This was just the way things were with Chip. He was always going out on a limb, but God always had a way of looking out for him. Actually, God seemed to always be out on that limb with him, taking care of him. We should have been more careful not to spend every last dollar on our honeymoon. But that favor from that sweet man made us feel as if maybe some things were just meant to be.

By the light of day, we went back to the yellow house full of hot stink, and I made up my mind right then and there to make the best of it. I pulled myself together and rolled up my sleeves (as people say), and I said to Chip, "Okay. Let's do this."

What else could I do? This was our home now. We didn't have any other options. I covered my nose and mouth and started cleaning. Once the two of us got the worst of it out, Chip went off and took care of some business. There were rent checks in from his other houses that needed to be cashed, and as soon as we had a few dollars in hand, we hit the hardware store.

I had never done anything design-related at that point, but there was something very liberating about starting from scratch. We knew every room needed to be painted, all the carpet needed to come out, and all the hardwood floors needed to be refinished. And Chip gave me free rein to make that home whatever I wanted to make it.

To be honest, I didn't know what I wanted to make it, so I started with one basic idea: "I have, like, six favorite colors, so I'm going to paint every room one of those colors."

Once I got going, I decided that using different colors in every room wasn't enough for me. I wanted to make every room a different *theme*. I went with a nautical theme in the front room and decorated with a bunch of cheap sailboats and netting that I bought at a hobby store. The kitchen was French-inspired, so it was mustard yellow. Our bedroom was hotel-inspired—all white. The back room was Chip-inspired, so it was cedar and horns and cowhides. Every room was completely different.

We did every part of this renovation together with our bare hands. Chip restored all of the wood floors, all the tile work—everything. I was learning as we went, but I definitely did my part.

That house was gorgeous. Jo did an awesome job helping fix it up, and her ideas were great. There was a moment in the kitchen when I smarted off, though. I don't even remember what I said, to be honest, but Jo got real mad and started yelling. She was carrying this five-gallon bucket of primer. She slammed it down on the ground to make a point, and it splashed right back up in her face. It was dripping off her eyelashes and her nose.

Whenever something like that happened in my family, we'd all just laugh, you know? So I laughed, even though she was mad at me, and that made her even angrier. She started yelling again with the primer dripping all over, and I just had this moment where I looked at her and everything seemed to be going in slow motion and I thought, *I love this woman. She is tough! Oh, this is gonna work.*

That was our first real "fight," and even now we both agree it was our biggest. Chip had smarted off about something, so my blood was already boiling, but when I slammed that bucket down, Chip says I became a ninja—the kind you don't want to mess with. Yet he *still* laughed, against his better judgment. We joke about it now, like, "Well, I'm mad, but I'm not primer-in-the-face mad."

It would take us a few months to get everything in livable condition in that house, even though we were living there full-time. Looking back, I don't know how we did it, but I guess you have a lot more time and energy before there are kids in the picture. We were newlyweds. We had our whole lives ahead of us. And despite the rough start, we were still riding the excitement of our honeymoon and feeding off of that energy we seemed to have whenever we were together, which was basically all the time.

Chip never said no to any of my ideas. He was 100 percent on board for my various theme rooms. He spoiled me in that way. But it was more than that. Chip supported everything I wanted to do. He even supported my dreams. The two of us would dream together all the time, just lying in bed at night, imagining where we could go in life, talking about things we always wanted to do or see or accomplish.

Until I left home and went to do my internship in New York City, I honestly didn't know what I wanted to do. At some point in my teen years, I told my father that I wanted to take over his Firestone shop when he retired. I thought that was the right thing to do. I thought it would make him proud, as if I were the son he'd never had who would step into his shoes and carry on the successful business he'd created.

Then I went to Baylor and got interested in broadcast journalism. I loved the storytelling and the editing process, and I managed to get two years' worth of internships under my belt at our local CBS station, KWTX. Everyone said that if you wanted to make it in TV news you had to go to New York City to do it, so I went out on a limb and applied to the *Today* show, *Good Morning America*, and *48 Hours*. Those shows didn't have internship affiliations with Baylor at the time, so it was a long shot to say the least. I just went and did it on my own out of blind, naive ambition, I guess.

I had lived a pretty sheltered life up until then, so when *48 Hours* selected me, I was worried my parents might fight it. How could they let their little girl go to the big city by herself? But I was wrong. My protective parents not only supported my ambition, they paid for my apartment for those six months—a good thing, too, because it was fifteen hundred dollars a month for a room in a shared apartment with two other people!

As amazing as it was to live on West 57th Street and to work under a man as esteemed as Dan Rather, I quickly fell out of love with the news business while working that job. My job as an intern was to read the papers to find salacious stories, cold cases, or horrible crime stories to pitch to the senior editors. It was heavy.

While I fell out of love with TV news, I did fall in love with New York City. It was more than just wandering in and out of those lovely boutiques that I mentioned before. I was pretty homesick during those six months, and I especially missed my mother. So it was eye-opening and beautiful to see so many people in that big city who looked like my mom and me. It seemed that everywhere I looked there was a woman walking down the street who reminded me of her. It was so unlike growing up in Kansas and Texas. New York is where I finally began to appreciate all of the different cultures and truly began to fall in love with my Korean heritage.

It's difficult to put into words, but there was something about that experience that helped me find myself. I would go home every night and write about my experiences—what I'd seen, what I'd done, and some-times just about whatever I was thinking or feeling. And as I did that, something shifted in me. I started owning who I am, realizing that I was unique and that God had a unique purpose for me. I'd spent my whole life worrying about what people thought about me or whether I was good enough or thinking about what I *should* be doing instead of really dig-ging down to find out what I *wanted* to do.

I had always been a religious person. I was brought up in the church, and my parents were very committed to getting the family there every Sunday without fail. So from the age of five to about twenty, religion to me was a matter of "you do this, and you don't do that, and you do your best to walk the straight line."

I was good at that. I'm good at following the rules—most of the time. But once I was on my own in New York, my faith became something very personal. It was no longer about what my parents knew or what my pastor knew. I came to think of God as more of a gracious friend who was accompanying me on this journey, a friend who wanted to carry my burdens and speak into my life and shape me into who I really was and who I would become.

When I came back to Waco, I had a very different perspective. I went back to work at my father's Firestone shop knowing that I didn't want to do broadcast journalism, but also doubting whether or not I wanted to take over the tire business. I spent a good part of my days in that back office daydreaming and sketching ideas out on a yellow steno pad.

I wasn't sure I wanted to run my dad's business, but I definitely liked the idea of owning my own business. I thought about what kind of business I'd like to own—a spa, a bakery, a home store. Whatever I chose, I wanted it to be as beautiful and welcoming as those boutiques in New York.

I drew pictures of what the shops might look like. I designed logos. I never shared those ideas with anybody, and there were times when I thought I was just being foolish. In fact, I started to think about my degree and the fact that I'd worked at one of the top evening news programs in all of television, and I wondered if maybe I'd given up on TV news too soon. I wondered if maybe I should go back to New York and go for it. I was actually in the middle of pulling up all the old contacts I'd made during my internship on the very day I met Chip at the tire shop.

And so I stayed in Waco, and my life took a sharp turn down a path I never could've imagined.

We'd only been living in the yellow house for about a month when I flipped open that yellow pad and showed Chip some of my ideas. Remodeling and redecorating that house had filled me with all sorts of new inspiration, so I showed him the sketches and plans I had made for a little home décor shop. I told him I wanted to apply everything I'd learned from this house and my days wandering around Manhattan to a business idea I'd been playing around with.

"Someday," I said.

"Why not right now?" Chip replied.

"What do you mean?"

"Go drive around and find a building you like, and let's do it. We'll fix it up just like we're fixing up this house, and you can open your business right now."

"Are you serious?"

"Of course I'm serious! Go find a building and let's do it! Why not?"

Chip had this way of turning far-off dreams into something that seemed real and achievable in an instant. He filled me up with a confidence I'd never known. He made me believe I could actually do it.

So I did.

I drove around Waco with new eyes, searching around every corner and strip mall for something that I could turn into my vision. One day, I spotted this little building on Bosque (pronounced BOSS-key) Boulevard. It was sunburnt orange—a bit like Chip on our first date—and it was all boarded up, but it looked more like a little house than a cookie-cutter, strip-mall type of business. It backed up to a residential neighborhood, it had its own little parking lot, and it was right next door to a church. There was something cute and quirky about the place that just caught my eye.

It wasn't for sale. It basically looked abandoned. But I took a picture on my phone and sent it to Chip.

"I love this building!" I told him.

His response was, "Jo, that thing is ugly."

"But I love all the windows, and I can imagine these pretty displays . . ."

I've picked some dumps, some buildings that weren't pretty, either. But this place seemed like it was on the wrong side of town for a retail location. It looked more like a place that you'd turn into a little gas station or a used car lot or something.

Chip didn't feel good about it, but he did some research anyway and found out the property was owned by a woman named Maebelle, who was probably in her seventies at the time. We reached out to her, and she agreed to meet us at the building. She told us the whole history of the place. Her son had been renovating it for years, but he had gotten very sick and had never been able to finish. She'd received a couple of offers on the property, but she just wasn't ready to part with it yet—especially since those bidders wanted to turn it into a used car lot or something else she didn't want to see in the neighborhood. She and her son had been looking to open a tuxedo shop, and she was hoping for something along those lines.

We had a good talk with Maebelle, and she loved the idea that I'd be opening a shop I would run myself, that I had no interest in tearing down that little building her son had worked on for so long. Before we left, we told her we'd like to make an offer too, and she said that when the time came she would rather sell it to us than to the other folks.

So we got all excited. Thinking back, maybe we got excited a little too quickly. Because we'd never thought through exactly how we'd finance the place.

I had a line of credit that worked well for flipping houses. It was a short-term thing. But I didn't have the credit needed to do a long-term commercial purchase like that. Even though this was gonna be Jo's business, it made sense to both of us that it should be in both our names.

I had a tiny bit of savings tucked away that I decided I could use for a down payment. I'd never thought I would touch that money, but Chip inspired me to want to do something more with it than just let it sit in the bank earning next to nothing in interest. I also knew that if I filled out a loan application, I'd still be able to show the income I'd been making at my dad's shop. I might even be able to qualify for some kind of small-business loan available to women. We decided to go for it and were excited to hear about some financing options Chip hadn't used before.

The bottom line was that I loved Jo, she loved me, and we loved being together. Working together energized us—it just worked out best. And no matter what it took, I was going to make this little shop work for her. When she shared that little yellow notepad of sketches with me, I knew this was like Jo sharing her diary or something. These were her innermost thoughts and dreams. I couldn't help but push her toward them. And the quicker, I thought, the better. No time to chicken out. Just like our first date.

After doing all the paperwork and scraping together as much as I could, I offered Maebelle $45,000 for her property. And she said, "Oh my. I've already had two offers for considerably more than that." She had thought we would come closer to those other offers, and she'd been sure she'd pick us over them, even if we came in a little under, simply because she liked us. But $45,000 was just too low.

"I am so sorry. I thought you guys were going to be a little closer," she said.

"I am so sorry if I offended you, Maebelle. That's just what I have," I said.

"Well, if you could come up with more, call me," she replied. "If not, I'm going to have to move on with these other people."

I knew we couldn't come up with more. Putting together the financing on that $45,000 was a stretch as it was. That was that.

I was really sad about it, of course. I'd managed to get all excited imagining the possibilities for what I could do in that location. I'd envisioned that shop from top to bottom. I swear I could smell the candles burning inside and see the looks on my customers' faces when they found that perfectly unique item that would fit in that perfect spot in their home.

I wasn't ready to give up. I knew we could probably find another location somewhere. But it was very hard to let go of the store I'd envisioned in that quirky old building on Bosque.

So that night and just about every night after that, I prayed: "Lord, that's the building that spoke to me. And if it's meant to be, please make it come back around."

# FIVE

## OPENING UP

Sometimes the thing we're dreaming of doesn't work out. But Chip and I weren't going to give up on the idea of opening my shop just because the building I fell in love with seemed to slip through our fingers. So we kept on looking for other buildings. We searched and searched, but nothing we found had the character and charm of that little spot on Bosque.

I was starting to lose hope when, a few weeks into our renewed search, my prayers were suddenly answered. Maebelle called me on my cell phone: "Joanna, I've been praying about it, and I do not know why, but I feel very strongly that God is saying I need to sell this building to you for $45,000."

I could hardly believe it. God made it so evident that this was meant to be. I was about to open my very own business!

Some friends and family members tried to talk me out of doing this. They felt it was just too big of a risk to take because I had no experience running a business of my own, no training in retail sales or marketing. I had never owned property before. And I knew next to nothing about home décor or design. Truly, the only home decorating I'd ever done was in the house where we were currently living, and that had just been one big experiment for me.

But Chip did what Chip does and made all those facts, all that logic, seem irrelevant. He really did. He believed I could do it, and he was confident that what I didn't know, I could learn.

I think part of what originally drew me to TV journalism was that I was a curious observer of other people. I may have been the quiet girl, but I was always the one who watched how things worked and took everything in. I'd told Chip all about how things worked in those shops in New York. Time spent by shoppers in those little boutiques was a sensory experience, and the store owners made sure of it. Women, especially, notice these kinds of details: the sweet smell of a candle burning, the color of a fresh bouquet of flowers next to the register, the music softly playing in the background, the allure of an interesting display—all of those things I'd mentioned earlier. As a shopper and a careful observer, I was able to appreciate the creative process that went into each little table and window installation.

In that sense, I wanted to create a store that was an experience, not just a collection of things for people to buy. I wanted to design it with intention and be sure I set things up to catch the eye of my shoppers. I also wanted to make sure my displays were practical and inspired my visitors to know that they, too, could set up their homes like this. My goal was to make design relatable, to make it attainable.

We took some time renovating that little houselike shop while I finished up our remodeling at home, and in the process I started collecting inventory. I bought inexpensive merchandise at the Dallas Market Center, an incredible wholesale marketplace filled with items sourced from all over the world. I hit garage sales and flea markets, too, and found old mirrors and furniture and knickknacks that I could fix up or distress to make them more appealing while adding some value to them.

At one point I found a large brown wicker sleigh for five bucks. I couldn't believe how cheap it was. I thought to myself, *If I dress this thing up a bit, I could sell it for twenty-five dollars.* Off to the local craft store I went. I found a fake ivy garland to wrap all around the sleigh and some battery-operated Christmas lights that I tucked into the ivy. I was so proud of the way it turned out that I thought maybe I could sell it before the shop even opened and get a taste for how this would all work. So I talked my father into putting it in his waiting area at Firestone with a price tag on it.

But a week went by, and I noticed the sleigh was still there. The second week, I called my dad. "Yes, JoJo, it's still here. But don't worry. It will sell." The third week went by, and I told my dad that if it didn't sell, I would just come pick it up and get it out of his way. At that point I felt deflated. I questioned more than ever if running a store was what I was supposed to be doing. But I went in toward the end of that third week, and my father handed me an envelope with twenty-five dollars in it. "I told you it would sell," he said. "Now go buy something for twenty dollars and see if you can sell it for fifty bucks. This is how retail works, JoJo."

Selling that sleigh made me feel like I could do this design thing despite the odds—and my lack of experience. But the more I shopped for bargains that I could turn around for profit, the harder it was to choose between what I wanted to sell and what I wanted to use to finish turning our house into a home over on Third Street.

It took nearly eight months to get it to a point where that yellow house finally felt finished. I was so happy to be done, to be free of the dust and debris and tools everywhere, and to finally get the place neatened up and livable. I don't like a lot of clutter. I like a clean house. If my house is too messy, I just can't think straight. And remodeling a house is messy by definition. So nearly eight months after being carried into a house full of rotten meat and dog urine, I was thrilled to finally have a place where we could be comfortable. I was proud of what we'd done too. I hoped we'd live there for a long time, and I was ready to focus all of my energies on the shop.

Then Chip came home one afternoon and said, "Hey, Jo, I bought a new house."

"Oh," I said. "To rent out?"

"Well, eventually, yeah. We're gonna be able to rent this house out now, because we fixed it up. It's ready to go. So let's move down to this next house a few doors down and we'll fix that one up, too, as nice as we made this one. We'll be able to make better rent on everything if we make 'em all look this good."

As I rode down the street with him to see what he'd bought, I was in shock when he pulled up in front of this tiny white box of a house. I mean *tiny*—maybe eight hundred square feet. There was no cute front porch. The yard—front and back—was all weeds and overgrown bushes. When he opened the front door on that cabin-size house, I could see it hadn't been touched in thirty years.

She cried. Again. That was sort of her thing during year one. If we ever write a marriage book, chapter 1 will be called, "She cried."

Chip assured me this was the right thing to do. This was how we were going to get ahead and make real money. He tried to remind me of the fun I'd had fixing up the yellow house, and I had to admit that some parts of it had been fun. I'd loved coming up with the themes for the rooms, and picking out all the colors and textures, and learning how to do the work myself. But the yellow house wasn't just some house to me after doing all of that work. It was *my* house. It was our *home*.

But Chip never saw it like that. He really never got attached to anything that didn't have a heartbeat. These houses, they were just inventory to him. He liked messing with them, but he certainly didn't want to live in any of them forever.

Even though he didn't understand why I was upset, he was smart enough to just leave me alone for a little while. I went back home and sat on the porch and thought, *How can we just rent this house out to college kids? My house.* We'd only been in there eight months. Then I got to thinking about how much work it had been, and the idea of starting from scratch again seemed daunting, especially with everything I was trying to do to get the shop opened up. I cried it out until I reached a point where I realized there was nothing much I could do about it. *He's already bought it, so we're kind of in this now. No one is going to rent that little white house out in the condition it's in.*

One thing I learned there on that beautiful front porch was if I wanted to be successful, if I wanted to do important work one day, I would have to increase my capacity. I had to learn to manage disappointment. I needed to learn how to make the most out of those "opportunities" Chip seemed to keep finding.

So I told Chip okay. We rented our house out that very week to some college students and moved ourselves down the block. We started renovating again. And because this house was half the size and I was already actively out there looking for inventory for the shop, it didn't take nearly as long to get everything finished.

We did suffer a few setbacks, like the time Chip decided to surprise me by using maroon grout on the white tile in the kitchen. He could tell I didn't like it the moment I walked in the room, and he wound up ripping it all out and doing it all over again. I'm not sure why I had such clear ideas about what I liked and didn't like, but I did. And the funny thing is that after a couple of months, once I had put my stamp on it, I was as much in love with that little house as I had been with the yellow one.

She jokes to this day, "I liked that house because I could vacuum the whole place without ever unplugging the cord."

I could plug into one outlet and vacuum every room! I loved that. It's true.

Back at my shop, the one thing I was having a hard time designing was a sign for the front of the building.

Chip and I had decided together that our little shop would be named Magnolia. I've always loved magnolia trees and their blooms—there's something so beautiful about a magnolia blossom. It demands attention, and you can't help but love those big, creamy petals and that fragrant smell. We'd handed out magnolia leaves at our wedding, and we'd had those two beautiful magnolia trees in the front yard of our first home together, so magnolias have always seemed like a part of us. Plus, they just seemed so entirely Southern. They reminded me of drinking sweet tea on the big wraparound porch of a nineteenth-century plantation home or something.

The name *Magnolia* just fit my business and the feeling I wanted to create. We loved it. But I really struggled with how to put the name on that sign. I figured I would have to hand-paint the thing since I didn't have a budget to have anything professionally made, and I just couldn't come up with anything that worked. I kept drawing things out, trying to write the word *Magnolia* in different ways, using the flower itself in a logo of sorts, and it just never felt right to me.

Then one day Chip showed up with the back of his pickup truck just loaded with old metal letters he'd found at a flea market—big, oddly shaped letters taken from various old signs. They were mismatched and rusty and dented—and I loved them. We tacked them up on the front of the shop, spelling out the name that would come to mean so much: *Magnolia*. The letters were uneven and looked a little handmade and ragged, but it seemed to work. I loved this sign because Chip designed it and made it with his own two hands. It came together in such an imperfectly perfect way, and I hoped people would get it.

To this day that sign is one of my proudest accomplishments. I'm no Joanna Gaines, but I certainly see things differently and love design in my own unique way. That first sign really reflected that for me. I would glow when I would hear a customer come in the shop and say, "I saw the sign and just had to stop in."

Finally, in October of 2005, the shop was ready to go. In a rush, I hand-painted a dinky little "Open" sign, but I ran out of space for the *n*, so it dropped down at the end. It was just bad. I didn't have an advertising budget. I hadn't done any marketing at all. We'd told plenty of people we knew, of course, and our parents had spread the word, but I was basically hoping that people would see my store when they were driving by and drop in. And yet I put out a sign on my opening day that looked like a four-year-old had drawn it. It was pathetic.

Inside, the shop was pretty much everything I wanted it to be. In addition to the home décor items, I had a section full of fresh flowers for sale. They smelled so good and looked perfect. When I was in New York, I had lived next to a little flower shop, and I'd loved watching people walk out with fresh flowers wrapped in kraft paper. I wanted to create that same feel in Waco, Texas that I had experienced in New York City.

So I had the flowers all ready to go. I had the candles burning. I had Frank Sinatra music playing. And at 9:55 a.m., just five minutes before the doors opened, I started to freak out.

She was hyperventilating. No joke. I thought I might have to take her to the emergency room or something, she was so nervous.

I just started panicking. "No one's going to come. Why is no one here?"

Chip and I had done the math. I needed to make at least two hundred dollars a day in order to pay the mortgage and insurance and electricity. That was two hundred dollars every day we were open just to stay afloat, without any profits. I'd been working so hard getting everything ready that I hadn't stopped to think about what might happen if the store didn't make that much money. I was close to a complete nervous breakdown, thinking, *What if this doesn't work?*

Then, just after ten o'clock, a Hummer pulled into the parking lot, followed by a Mercedes, followed by a Suburban and then a BMW. All these rich women showed up out of nowhere.

They were doctors' and lawyers' wives, stay-at-home moms and grandmothers who loved to shop and who did their best to make their homes feel nice. It turned out they'd all been watching my little shop come together during the renovations. They'd been eagerly anticipating my opening day for weeks, and it seemed that my idea of bringing a New York-style boutique experience to a home décor store wasn't far-fetched at all. There were a lot of people in town who were excited for it.

My first day open we made $2,800.

By the way, my dad decided to sell his Firestone shop shortly after this. I went over and helped him clean out the attic one day, and guess what I found up there? The wicker sleigh that I'd fixed up nice with the garland and Christmas lights and put up for sale in his lobby was still there, tucked in a corner. I just shook my head. He bought it himself to give me a little boost of confidence as I got ready to open my store.

What can I say? It worked. And so did the shop.

Sometimes when something is meant to be, it's meant to be. It had nothing to do with how I advertised, and it certainly didn't have anything to do with my being some kind of an amazing designer or having a reputation, because I wasn't any kind of a designer at all, and no one knew who I was. I just knew what I liked, and I trusted that other people might like it too. And I was where I was supposed to be. I'd listened to my own intuition and let God guide me toward the plans he'd had for me all along.

I mean, is there anyone who could possibly imagine that the way to get to your life's calling would be to marry a guy who showed up an hour and a half late to your first date and then to let that man talk you into opening your own small business in the first year of marriage? But guess what? It all seemed to be working out in that perfectly messy way life works when you trust in God and his plans for your life rather than focusing on your own.

At that point, I wasn't anywhere near used to the dynamics of it all. Chip's impulsive buying of properties, the way I'd hate them at first and then come to love them, only to have to move out again, the unexpected twists and turns and the hardships we'd have to overcome to get ourselves back on course—all of that was still new to me. And as we repeated them over the next few years, moving from flip house to flip house and starting over again and again, there would be a whole lot of tears.

But the fact that we established that crazy pattern of doing things in our own unique way so early on in our marriage was important. It prepared us for everything that would come later on. And Chip's decision to move us into that little white eight-hundred-square-foot house worked out exactly the way he said it would. It helped us to get ahead and start making some sustainable income.

One of the real pluses to that second house was it had a big side yard that we could subdivide, so we could build a whole second house to rent or to sell right next to the one we were living in. I bought that house, lot included, for $30,000, and we probably put $25,000 into it. So we were all-in for $55,000 on that little house, and it turned out beautiful—it really did. And we were able to build a brand-new house next door for about $130,000.

And of course this was all debt. We didn't own anything outright. And getting the money to do all this hadn't been easy. The banks hadn't wanted to mess around with these little houses at first. They were either small potatoes, or the banks felt I needed to build a reputation first. The few they actually agreed to caused us to go scrambling every month just to make the payments and pay our own bills.

When it came to remodeling, we never took out any walls or did any major construction at that point. Everything was just cosmetic. But we tried to do things creatively and nice. We updated the kitchen with new appliances. We used the existing cabinets and learned to repaint them. We put in new countertops and a new backsplash when we could. We restored the hardwood floors, and I mean lots of them. Chip literally became an expert in setting tile and wood floor restoration. We took out the bathtub and replaced it with a nice, wide shower with multiple showerheads and some body jets. Honestly, it felt luxurious, like the kind of shower you'd find in a really upscale house or a spa somewhere. Then came the paint, and we were done. And by that point, as I've mentioned, I would be in love with the place.

But it wasn't just the work we put in that made me love that tiny white house. It wasn't even the easy vacuuming, though that was a plus. What made that house special was the incredible memories we made there.

We threw Chip's thirtieth birthday party in that house's little back-yard. I strung Christmas lights in the trees, and Chip built a firepit that was unbelievable. We didn't have much in the way of backyard furniture, so I put hay bales all around the perimeter for people to sit on. There was a little old weathered shed in the back, and I lit that up too.

It looked like something you'd see in a magazine. It was one of the best parties I've ever had in my life. It was funny because we were basically poor. We didn't know how we were going to pay our bills at the end of the month, and we were living in this tiny house, and I invited all of these college buddies to my party who'd gone and started making real money. They came in from Dallas and Austin and parked their Beemers and their Range Rovers up on the lawn of this $30,000 property we owned.

But we were proud of that house. We didn't think anything of it. We were excited to have all of our friends from college there to see what we'd been up to and to celebrate Chip's thirtieth birthday together.

I was thirty years old and still living by the seat of my pants. I probably should have had my life together a little bit more by then. But the thing was, my friends all had these stressed-out lives, and they came to our place and it felt like we were just living this laid-back, beautiful, no-stress life. We made being poor look fun. All these cor-porate friends of ours were thinking, *Well, maybe it wouldn't have been so bad to stay in Waco.*

It wasn't just my friends that made that party special, though. My grandma was still alive, and she came to that party too. She was just the sweetest lady in the world. She had single-handedly raised my dad and his brother. And though she had a very tough life, you would have never known it by her attitude. Between my mom and my grandma, I was definitely genetically built for positive optimism. That day with her is one of my fondest memories, because she and I hung out on one of those bales of hay for what felt like hours. It wasn't but a couple years after that she went to be with Jesus.

We made all kinds of big memories in that tiny house, and we were just getting started. The fact that we had some profits starting to roll in from my little shop on Bosque only added to the sense of security we were building.

It's hard to describe the feeling that comes with starting your own business. It really is so much work in the beginning that you lose yourself in it. You lose your sense of time, and you can't believe how quickly the days go by because there's no time to focus on much of anything else. But then you open the doors, and it's like you've given birth to this new thing that didn't exist before. Then when it starts to flourish, well, that's just icing on the cake. To get to see it live and breathe and to know that this thing you created out of thin air can put a smile on other people's faces is such a blessing.

There were some women who would come into that store and drop fifteen hundred dollars in a single visit. It was unbelievable. But I think one of the favorite customers I had in that first year of Magnolia was a woman who didn't ever buy a thing. She would just show up now and then and poke around, and she told me one time, "I just come here because I want to be in here. This place inspires me."

That was just about the greatest compliment I could ever imagine. She affirmed for me that I had accomplished exactly what I'd set out to do, and that made me even more passionate about creating an experience for my customers. I worked every day to come up with new touches that would make the experience memorable. I never got too comfortable with one particular look or design. I wanted to constantly challenge myself and make it better. If people were going to go out of their way to come into my store, I wanted to make sure it was worthwhile, whether they bought something or not.

Magnolia was my baby—no doubt about that. But it wasn't long before I found out it wasn't the only baby I was going to have.

# SIX

# WHITE PICKET FENCES

I've been asked from time to time how Chip and I manage to juggle all the things we did—and still do. I honestly don't have a good answer for that, other than to go back to the notion that we seem to energize one another when we're together. Although one explanation for where we find a little "extra" time in our days is the fact that since we got married we have never had a TV in our own house.

That is one question I always field on Twitter, "Hey man, why doesn't Joanna ever set up a TV in any of these homes?" I think they are implying I need to turn in my man card. But this is actually the answer to that question.

Before we got married, the two of us attended a few premarital counseling sessions with Chip's friend and one of his mentors, Byron Weathersbee, and his wife, Carla. Byron had played a significant part in Chip's life as a college student, and since then, Chip sought Byron's wisdom on lots of things. Chip and I felt that applying that same logic to our marriage—getting advice from these two trusted and seasoned marriage pros—couldn't be a bad thing. We wanted to start a habit of seeking outside opinions just to make sure we were thinking about everything a new couple ought to think about as we started our new life together.

One of the things Byron and Carla suggested was that we try to stay focused on each other and spend quality time doing things we loved together, especially when we were at home. That seemed like a no-brainer to us, but they explained that being in the same house and actually *interacting* with each other are two different things. Sometimes it's easy for couples to get lost in their own little worlds at home—to be so focused on other things that they aren't really together, even when they're in the same room.

To counter that tendency, Byron and Carla suggested we try to go the first few weeks of our marriage without a TV. The idea was to find other ways to occupy our time, especially in the evenings, with activities we could truly share. It seemed like reasonable advice, and so we tried it.

Well, six months later, neither one of us had the slightest urge to get a TV. We never even found time to miss it. All our various projects kept us busy during the day. And our evenings were pretty filled up with making dinner and finishing up the day's business, talking and dreaming together, and making plans for the next day or the next week. We couldn't imagine setting aside even an hour to sit and watch TV.

That's not to say we never slowed down. Reading a good book, flipping through magazines, learning new card games together, taking walks together—we found a million ways to enjoy some down time.

Now, to be fair, we've caught our share of TV at our friends' homes or at our parents'. Any time there was a big game or a fun show, we would find a way to catch it at a restaurant or make a date of it at a friend's house. So, we managed to catch up on some of our favorite shows through these outlets.

We've had more than thirteen years now without a TV, and I don't feel like we've missed a thing.

Just when we thought our lives couldn't get any busier—just as we'd settled into that little white house and my store was getting off the ground—I received the wonderful news that I was pregnant with our first child.

Just the thought of having a baby filled me with all sorts of new inspiration, not the least of which was imagining the room I wanted my baby to come home to. The tiny second bedroom in that eight-hundred-square-foot house needed a complete makeover to turn it into a nursery, and thinking about that actually spurred an idea that gave me a new perspective on decorating.

I had made the décor in our second home more cohesive than the ones in the yellow house. The colors were continuous, and the rooms all tied together rather than each space having its own theme. My store was so busy that I kept finding new furnishings and swapping them in and out between the store and our home, and I felt like I was starting to get a hang of this thing called decorating.

Once I found out I was having a boy, I zeroed in on earthy tones and a sort of outside-meets-inside theme in the room. Instead of the standard baby blue, I wanted something warm and comfortable that would reflect the rest of that luxurious little retreat we'd created. But I didn't have a lot of money to spend on that little nursery. Any money we made seemed to go right into another project or investment or just to keep up the payments on all the loans we'd taken out.

I realized we just couldn't afford any extra bells and whistles on that room, not even window treatments. I knew that window treatments can be expensive. But I decided to look at our tiny budget as a design challenge. I stood in the nearly finished nursery one day, just staring out the window, and I noticed the little white picket fence we'd put up in the front yard. An idea popped into my head immediately, "Hey, Chip, what would happen if you went and got some pieces of picket fence at the lumberyard and built an awning out of that wood for the inside of the nursery?"

I sketched it out for him, with the picket fence coming down at an angle from above the windows, kind of like an awning you'd see on the outside of a restaurant. Chip ran with it and figured out how to tack fencing to another board so he could hang it just so. We painted it, and it worked!

I stood back when we were done, looked at that room, and realized something big: having a tight budget doesn't have to mean watering down the design. If anything, it forced me to get *more* creative, and there was so much joy in that for me. I loved that awning Chip built way more than I ever would've loved a store-bought window treatment. It turned out perfect and taught me one of my fundamental design rules: don't be afraid to think outside of the box.

People liked those awnings so much that we actually started building them and selling them to our clients. For a season those things were hot!

Well, that was the other thing that happened. Beyond the house flipping and rental properties, we started picking up clients for remodels and redesigns.

As my baby bump grew behind the counter at the store, I found that more and more of those moms and grandmothers who came in to browse started bringing me pictures of rooms in their homes and asking for my advice. "I just don't like this room, and I don't know why," they would say. I would look at those pictures and suggest that maybe they could switch the furniture around or put up something interesting on a wall that had nothing but flat picture frames on it. I would recommend changing the wall color or adding a nice lamp in a nook or adding new throw pillows for a pop of color on the sofa.

It was a new challenge daily, but giving the advice sharpened my design skills, and I learned a few things about my own style in the process. It was an education for me. But more than that, it started to evolve into a second business.

Occasionally I'd point out that a room called for much more than new throw pillows, and the owner would ask, "Well, is that something you could do for me? I'd love to just hire you and Chip to come in and do the work!"

Between building the new house on our newly subdivided lot, continuing work on some small flip homes, and managing the rentals, Chip had more work than he could do himself, so he had put a crew of workmen together. "The Boys," as we called them, were a talented bunch of hardworking guys who were just as adaptable as Chip seemed to be when it came to making my crazy ideas become reality. I truly could say, "Hey, why don't we take that tree out of the front yard and hang it upside down in the master bedroom," and they would do it, no questions asked. (All right, maybe there'd be a little head scratching. But then they'd shrug their shoulders and get to work.) So between all of us, we picked up this occasional additional work doing interiors—painting, refinishing floors, basically redecorating for these new clients.

It wasn't easy to juggle it all, especially since I was running the store by myself that first year. But I loved every minute of it. There was no doubt in my mind that I was doing what I was meant to be doing.

---

I wonder sometimes if we know ourselves a lot better than we think we do when we're children. We get into our teen years and college years, and so many of us let others redefine who we are, or we get lost along the way and have no idea what we really want to do with our lives. But once we finally figure it out, it often seems easy to look back into our childhoods and find a few clues that say, "Hey, maybe you were headed in that direction all along."

For me, the entrepreneurial spirit was always there. During my young years in Wichita, Kansas, my mom worked at a little gift shop owned by one of her friends. After school my two sisters and I would go there while she worked, and I would always play store. I would sit there and pretend that I was working the cash register. I would have my sisters bring stuff up to the counter, and I would wrap it. I loved doing that. Even when we'd go home, I would set up my whole room like a store and then have fake customers come in. At one point I had a set of Lee Press-On Nails, and I would make my sisters come in like customers to a spa. I was always thinking about ways to make money, so I would basically make my sisters pay me for whatever they were buying, even if it was only a dime.

On the weekends I made a habit of setting up these makeshift little carnivals in our backyard and charging neighborhood kids a dollar to get in. I'd have lemonade and rides (primarily just the swing set) and games. To swing on the swing set would cost you another dime. But I always wanted it to be this fun experience for everyone, so I would work hard all week getting it set up.

My sisters basically provided free labor for me, in addition to having to pay to get in. I'm not sure why they went along with it, seeing that I was the middle child, but they did. Home was the place where I asserted myself, and I wasn't shy about it the way I was in other places. I felt safe at home and felt like I could be me.

I was also a creative kid, but not in terms of artistry or design or anything like that. I was just always pretending. I kept trying to invent wings so I could fly. I always wanted to come up with something that someone would buy. So I was always thinking.

I remember playing a lot by myself. My older sister and my younger sister, when they weren't being my minions, were usually out playing with the neighborhood kids, but I could usually be found in a corner playing make-believe. I pretended different things at different phases of my childhood. For a while I was always doing pretend commercials. So if I were eating breakfast, I would hold up the cereal box and say, "Kellogg's. We make this nutritious." I would read it like a newscaster and pretend that I was on a commercial. Sometimes I'd do the same thing with the bottle of shampoo in the shower. No matter where I was, I would act out these commercials as if I had a real audience.

That's another strange thing, considering what I'm doing now. Growing up, I sometimes felt like this audience of mine was always with me, watching me in my pretend store, watching me doing commercials. It was almost as if I was living in the *Truman Show,* that movie with Jim Carrey in which a character is filmed from the moment of birth and watched by millions as he goes through his daily life. Even if I was by myself, I would look around and think, *I know you are out there watching me.*

My parents remember hearing me talking to this unseen audience often when I was a little girl. They say I also swore I had a pet rabbit named Jo. But according to my parents, it was just make-believe. It was all the expression of a creative mind.

Anyway, looking back, I can see there were a whole bunch of things in my childhood that pointed toward what I'd do in my adult life. And once I started doing it "for real," I thrived. It seemed that the more opportunities I had to get creative and get entrepreneurial, the more fulfilled and energized I felt about life.

Outside of the store, Chip and I kept most of our endeavors in our typical wheelhouse. We sank our money and time into Third Street, where Chip continued to be the honorary "mayor" as he continued to expand his rental and home-building business.

A big part of Chip's dream for that street began in a deal he made before we were married. Chip and his father went in on a deal together to purchase eleven acres of land just a few blocks from where we would live as newlyweds. Chip was convinced that the Third Street area would go up in value. Baylor University was only about a mile away, just across La Salle Avenue. And eventually, Chip believed, Baylor would run out of room to house its growing student population.

Well, his intuition on that was right. A big out-of-town company came along and saw what Chip was doing with his few small rental houses in this mostly untouched area of Waco, and they made him an offer—a good offer—on those eleven acres. Their plan was to build hundreds of units of dorm-style apartment homes on Third Street to market to the Baylor community. They were basically going to create a whole new neighborhood on the land Chip and his dad had been sitting on.

Chip wasn't interested in selling all the land off. He had big dreams of owning rental homes up and down Third Street. So he structured a deal that sold off the back part of the acreage to that big company, while he kept the acreage along the road frontage to split into small lots where he could eventually build some individual rental houses himself.

Chip and his father made good money on that sale, and that allowed us to do some more investing, hire more help, and get started building some more little rental homes—basically sinking every penny that came into our long-term future. In our personal lives, we were still barely scraping by. But the business side of things was going well. In fact, we were seeing so much growth and progress on Third Street that there were times when we felt as if the whole neighborhood was ours.

Only it wasn't.

By this time we had three dogs—Shiner, Maggie, and Blue, all rescue mutts. It was too crowded in an eight-hundred-square-foot house to keep three dogs inside all the time, so we'd let those dogs out to roam around. They were a lot like me and pretty much thought they owned Third Street too. I had this four-wheeler that I'd ride up and down the street, just checking on everything, and those dogs would run right along with me.

They were some of the best dogs you've ever seen. They never bothered anyone, certainly never bit anyone or even came close. But we had this one neighbor across the street who hated those dogs, and every single time she saw them off leash—which was just about all the time—she called animal control.

The people from the pound would show up, haul the dogs downtown in their van, and write us a ticket either in Jo's name or my name. There were times when the officer would call the dogs right off of our front porch: "Come here, dogs!" They'd hop right in his van, and off they'd go, back for another stay in the pound.

These weren't like parking tickets either. They came with heavy fines, which I absolutely refused to pay out of some misguided form of principle. I never was much of a rule follower, and this "put your dog on a leash" rule was no exception. If the dogs had been hurting somebody, I'd have understood. But to take them from our own front yard?

Well, guess what? When you don't pay your fines, eventually the police come looking for you.

We owed something like twenty-five-hundred dollars in tickets, and we simply didn't have that kind of money lying around, even if we wanted to pay the fines. Especially since I was about to have a baby. Sure enough, two weeks early, I delivered a beautiful, healthy baby boy that we named Drake. We named him after the New York hotel where we'd stayed on our honeymoon.

So Drake was a week old, and I was sitting in this house, feeding him in the back room, when I heard a knock on the door. Chip answered it. It was the police.

"Is Joanna Gaines here? We have a warrant here for her arrest," the officer said.

It was the tickets. I knew it. And I panicked. I picked up my son and I hid in the closet. I literally didn't know what to do. I'd never even had a speeding ticket, and all of a sudden I'm thinking, *I'm about to go to prison, and my child won't be able to eat. What is this kid gonna do?*

I heard Chip say, "She's not here."

Thankfully, Drake didn't make a peep, and the officer believed him. He said, "Well, just let her know we're looking for her," and they left.

Jo's the most conservative girl in the world. She had never even been late for school. I mean, this girl was straitlaced. So now we realize there's a citywide warrant out for her arrest, and we're like, "Oh, crap." In her defense, Jo had wanted to pay those tickets off all along, and I was the one saying, "No way. I'm not paying these tickets." So we decided to try to make it right. We called the judge, and the court clerk told us, "Okay, you have an appointment at three in the afternoon to discuss the tickets. See you then." We wanted to ask the judge if he could remove a few of them for us. The fines for our dogs "running at large" on our front porch just seemed a bit excessive.

We arrived at the courthouse, and Chip was carrying Drake in his car seat. I couldn't carry it because I was still recovering from Drake's delivery. We got inside and spoke to a clerk. They looked at the circumstances and decided to switch all the tickets into Chip's name.

Those dogs were basically mine, and it didn't make sense to have the tickets in her name. But as soon as they did that, this police officer walked over and said, "Hey, do you mind emptying out all of your pockets?"

I got up and cooperated. "Absolutely. Yep," I said. I figured it was just procedure before we went in to see the judge.

Then he said, "Yeah, you mind taking off your belt?"

I thought, *That's a little weird.*

Then he said, "Do you mind turning around and putting your hands behind your back?"

They weren't going to let us talk to the judge at all. The whole thing was just a sting to get us to come down there and be arrested. They arrested Chip on the spot. And I'm sitting there saying, "I can't carry this baby in his car seat. What am I supposed to do?"

I started bawling. "You can't take him!" I cried. But they did. They took him right outside and put him in the back of a police car.

Now I feel like the biggest loser in the world. I'm in the back of a police car as my crying wife comes out holding our week-old baby.

I'm walking out, limping, and waving to him as they drive away.

And I can't even wave because my hands are cuffed behind my back. So here I am awkwardly trying to make a waving motion with my shoulder and squinching my face just to try to make Jo feel better.

It was just the most comical thing, honestly. A total joke. To take a man to jail because his dogs liked to walk around a neighborhood, half of which he owns? But it sure wasn't funny at the time. I was flooded with hormones and just could not stop crying. They told me they were taking my husband to the county jail.

Luckily we had a buddy who was an attorney, so I called him. I was clueless. "I've never dated a guy that's been in trouble, and now I've got a husband that's in jail. What do I do? What's the first step here?" I asked. He made some calls, and he told me that I could get Chip out with a bail bond for eight hundred dollars.

It couldn't be done with a personal check, and we didn't have eight hundred dollars in the bank anyway. I needed eight hundred dollars in cash to go buy a money order at the gas station near the facility in order to get Chip out of jail, and I didn't have the money to do it. My parents or his parents would have given us that money in a heartbeat, I'm sure, but I was too embarrassed. I didn't want our parents to know we didn't have eight hundred dollars between us, and I certainly didn't want them knowing Chip was in the slammer.

Thankfully, I had my shop. I went and I emptied out both the cash register and the safe in the back. I didn't know how I'd make change the next day, and I had no idea how we'd make up for that loss when it came time to pay the bills. But I had no choice. It was the only money I had.

Off I went to the gas station. Then I went to the jail with my week-old son strapped to my chest in his BabyBjörn and waited. And waited.

Chip had been in there for a few very long hours. I had all kinds of awful thoughts about what might have happened to him in there. What if he'd been roughed up? Strip-searched? Who knows what awful things could have happened in a place like that? I saw scary-looking characters come and go as I sat in that cold, concrete lobby, trying to make myself invisible.

Finally, out came Chip.

"Hi, baby. Thanks for bailing me out," he said.

He sounded almost chipper.

"Are you okay?"

"Yeah, yeah! You'll never guess who I saw in there. Alfonzo! Remember the lawn guy who used to work for me? We had a good time catching up."

Only Chip could go to prison and come out talking about all the friends he'd run into there.

I came out and I was like, "Whoa! That was awesome. Jo, I met this guy. He did this thing. You know this old guy that I used to tell you about—he and I used to work together? He's doing great. Well, he's in jail, but things are really good otherwise."

Two of the policemen were also buddies of mine. These guys were literally standing on the other side of these bars going, "Why are you here? What's the deal?" We had this endearing conversation right there, while I was in a jail cell.

I used to live out in the boonies when I was in college, and I had mowed this one guy's grass. So I told him what I was in for. "Long story short, I got these dogs running around." And he was like, "Oh, dude, you'll be fine. I'm sure they'll get you right out of here."

It was just another day in my new life with Chip Gaines. But that was the moment I realized that we were right on the edge of a real financial struggle, and I didn't like that feeling.

I have a naturally conservative nature, and Chip and I were supposed to balance each other out, not concede to each other's strengths and weaknesses. My strength is saving and being tight with the money, but I had not exercised that strength recently. I had let my head get in the clouds and forgotten that this was important.

Not having the money to pay for those tickets in the first place should have been a wake-up call. Having to scrape the bottom of our barrel for bail money was certainly cause for alarm. I promised myself I would start putting money aside for future emergencies.

I don't think it's irrational or too conservative of me to think, *I never want to carry my baby into the county jail ever again.*

Is it?

# SEVEN

# ONE DOOR CLOSES

The very next week, I got back to work. I needed to get back in the shop and start making some sales to recoup the money we'd pulled out for bail and then to pay off the rest of those tickets. I didn't have a babysitter or the money to pay one. So I started working every day with a two-week-old baby.

We set up a little nursery area in the back office with a Pack 'n Play portable crib, and I worked the register with Drake in his BabyBjörn. I would run to the back office to feed him, and then, of course, a customer would walk in. So I'd have to wrap up the feeding session, which would make him cry.

I knew I needed to get some help at the shop. I couldn't do all of this by myself anymore.

Thank God for Jessica! She was a good friend from college, one of the two sets of twins in our wedding. And best of all, she was available. I hired her on to assist behind the register, and that gave me a little bit of freedom. Jessica had a way about her that made every customer feel warm and welcome. I was thankful for her diligence and friendship during that time when I was both a new mom and a new business owner.

Just as Drake turned six weeks old, I decided I wanted to lose some baby weight. Chip and I were both still getting used to the idea that we had a baby of our own now, but I felt it was okay to leave him with Chip for a half hour or so in the mornings so I could take a short run up and down Third Street. I left Drake in the little swing he loved, kissed Chip good-bye, and off I went.

Chip was so sweet and supportive. When I got back he was standing in the doorway saying, "Way to go, baby!" He handed me a banana and asked if I'd had any cramps or anything. I hadn't. I actually felt great.

I walked in and discovered Chip had prepared an elaborate breakfast for me, as if I'd run a marathon or something. I hadn't done more than a half-mile walk-run, but he wanted to celebrate the idea that I was trying to get myself back together physically. He'd actually driven to the store and back and bought fresh fruit and real maple syrup and orange juice for me.

I sat down to eat, and I looked over at Drake. He was sound asleep in his swing, still wearing nothing but his diaper. "Chip, did you take Drake to the grocery store without any clothes on?"

Chip gave me a real funny look. He said, "What?"

I gave him a funny look back.

"Oh my gosh," he said. "I totally forgot Drake was here. He was so quiet."

"Chip!" I yelled, totally freaked out.

I was a first-time mom. Can you imagine?

Anyone who's met Chip knows he can get a little sidetracked, but this was our child!

He was in that dang swing that just made him perfectly silent. I felt terrible. It had only been for a few minutes. The store was just down the street. But I literally got on my knees to beg for Jo's forgiveness.

Several days later I decided to go on a good long jog, trusting that Chip would not leave Drake again. As I was on my way back I saw Chip coming down the road in his truck with the trailer on it. He rolled up to me with his window down and said, "Baby, you're doing so good. I'm heading to work now. I've got to go."

I looked in the back, thinking, *Of course, he's got Drake.* But I didn't see a car seat.

"Chip, where's Drake?" she said, and I was like, "Oh, shoot!" She took off without a word and ran like lightning all the way back to the house as I turned the truck around. She got there faster on foot than I did in my truck.

I sure hope no one from Child Protective Services reads this book. They can't come after me retroactively, can they?

Chip promised it would never happen again. So the third time I attempted to take a run, I went running down Third Street and made it all the way home. I walked in, and Chip and Drake were gone. I thought, *Oh, good. Finally he remembered to take the baby.* But then I noticed his car was still parked out front. I looked around and couldn't find them anywhere.

Moments later, Chip pulled up on his four-wheeler—with Drake bungee-strapped to the handlebars in his car seat. "Chip!" I screamed, "What in the heck are you doing?"

"Oh, he was crying, and I'd always heard my mom say she would drive me around the neighborhood when I was a baby, and it made me feel better," Chip said. "He loved it. He fell right to sleep."

"He didn't love it, Chip. He probably fell asleep because the wind in his face made it impossible to breathe."

I didn't go for another run for the whole first year of Drake's life, and I took him to the shop with me every single day. Some people might see that as a burden, but I have to admit I loved it. Having him in that BabyBjörn was the best feeling in the world.

Drake was a shop baby. He would come home every night smelling like candles.

We had friends who owned a barbecue joint, and their baby always came home smelling like a rack of ribs. I liked Drake's smell a whole lot better.

A lot of my clientele seemed to have kids who were older, and I swear every single one of those moms would smile and coo over Drake, saying, "Joanna, this goes by so fast. You need to embrace these moments. My kids are getting ready to go off to college, and it feels like just yesterday they were little like this." And as much as they loved shopping at my store, some of my best customers kept saying, "You should think about taking some time off—maybe close up shop for a while. This is a moment in time you'll never get back. Don't work too much. Make sure you're all-in with your baby."

I didn't listen at first. What new mom does? It seems as if every day lasts forever when you're up all night with feedings and changing smelly diapers. But the more I heard those words, the more they started to sink in.

Toward the end of 2005, Chip came across an opportunity to buy a nice lot just up the road from where we lived. He knew how cramped we were in that little white house, and even though he felt as though any money we made should be reinvested in the business and rolled into the next project, he asked me one day if maybe we should invest in building a house of our own.

"Yes!" I said. I *loved* that idea.

Chip was pretty certain he could get the financing together for the house if we bought the land, but the parcel of land was $5,000, and he wasn't sure how we were going to get it before somebody else snatched it up.

That's when I surprised him. Ever since the jail incident, I had been saving a little money here and there from my sales at the shop. I just set it away where neither of us would touch it until there was something important to use it on, just for us.

The amount of money I had saved was exactly $5,000—just what we needed to buy that land. So we went for it, and together we designed a comfortable, sixteen-hundred-square-foot home from the ground up. I loved designing this home from the beginning stages.

I learned that, unlike the older homes we had renovated, a new home doesn't come with oak floors, thick trim, and built-in character. And I learned pretty quickly that adding character was expensive. If I wanted our place to be special and unique, I had to get creative. On the exterior, for instance, we wanted rock, but could only afford enough for the front of the house. So we added larger trees in the landscape to hide the side elevation and draw attention to the front door.

Speaking of that front door, Chip had to get creative himself. Buying things for clients was one thing, but buying stuff for our house was a different story. We had this charming arched door, crafted out of solid mesquite wood, that Chip had bought from a guy whose shop was going out of business. The best thing about this door was it had a peep door at the top that you could open so you could see who was on the other side. It felt very Hansel and Gretel. This amazing door brought the perfect balance to the heavy rock exterior—made it feel like a quaint rustic cottage.

On the inside, we couldn't afford the oak wood floors I loved, so we opted for stained concrete. I didn't want the room to look too cold, so we ended up scoring the concrete in a large diagonal pattern that made the floors look like a million bucks. We had some exterior rock left over, so I decided to mount the remaining pieces as a chair rail under our bar top, which Chip had constructed from reclaimed wood. Eventually it all came together, and we thought it was beautiful. It was so rewarding to stay on budget but have a house that was unique in its own special way.

In 2006 we moved in, and the layout worked so well that we decided our house would make the perfect model for a new set of student rental homes. We figured we could fit eight of those houses along the frontage parcels Chip had retained after selling part of the eleven acres to that big, out-of-town development company. But building those houses would mean getting a bigger line of credit and expanding Chip's ragtag home-building and house-flipping business into more of a bona fide company.

This house-building business quickly became more than Chip's company. It became *our* company, a true fusion of what he was doing and what I was doing. We decided to call it Magnolia Homes.

It was right around that time when I found out I was pregnant with our second child. This time it was going to be a girl. We decided to name her Ella Rose.

Sales at my shop were better in my second year than they'd been in the first. I was building a reputation and a steady client base, and I felt like I was starting to actually know what I was talking about in terms of design.

I loved that shop. I loved being there every day. Yet once I was pregnant with Ella, I heard a voice. Remember the voice on our first date, the one that told me Chip was the man I would marry? This was the same voice. But this time it was saying, *Jo, it's time to stay home with your babies.*

I didn't really want to hear that. In fact, I argued with the voice, just as I had argued about what it said about Chip. "No, I can't," I said. "I'm finally getting this! It's working!"

And it *was* working, better than I ever expected. That shop meant something to a lot of people, and I'm not just talking about me and my clientele.

It seemed that wherever we went and whatever we did, Chip would always find some kids to mentor along the way. One late night we were at the shop unboxing some candles that had just come in, and Chip noticed two young boys walking through our parking lot. They were all of ten years old.

"Hey, guys," he said. "It's late! What are you guys doing out here on the streets at this time of night?"

They said they lived in the neighborhood behind the shop, and they always walked around at night. So Chip said, "Hey, you want to make a little bit of money?"

Of course the boys said yes. He invited them to come help us with inventory and gave them work sweeping and doing some other chores for a few bucks an hour. We always seemed to find ourselves at the shop doing something late at night, so those boys started dropping by regularly. "Hey, Chip and JoJo!" they'd say. "Got any work for us?"

Being able to mentor those kids just added to the value of being at the shop. I loved that. It was such a good feeling to see those kids fired up about doing some work rather than wandering around after dark, where trouble was sure to find them.

What I'm trying to say is that I truly loved *everything* about that shop. But the voice just kept on telling me, *Jo, it's time.*

I wrestled with it for weeks until finally I felt it in my heart. I thought about the words of all of those women who were in my shop every day, telling me to cherish this time with my child. Soon I would have two children whose time deserved cherishing.

As much as I didn't want it to be true, I could no longer deny that the voice was right.

I'm the type of person who can wrestle with something for a long time, but when I finally make up my mind, I'm all-in. This was one of those times. I was lying in bed with Chip one night, and I spoke it out loud. I didn't pose it as a question. It wasn't something I needed advice on. I was resolved: "Chip, we're shutting the shop down."

Chip was curious as to why I had come to this decision, of course. And I told him confidently, "God told me to do it."

How could he argue with that?

In March of 2006 we sold off everything—the inventory, the displays, even the cash register. And it was *hard*. That shop was my dream, a dream that had landed on my yellow steno pad after I came back from my eye-opening internship in New York City. It was the first dream of mine that I'd seen come to fruition, and in many ways it was like our first baby.

Chip and I had remodeled that old shop with our bare hands. We'd laughed about how many nails had been driven into the old floorboards—there were thousands of them!—and thought about the guy who had put in so much time and effort all those years ago just to make sure those floors were as solid as could be. We were proud of everything we'd done to accentuate the work of those who came before us and to turn that quirky little building into a shop that exceeded the dreams I'd drawn out on paper a few years earlier.

But the shop was more to me than an accomplishment or even the fulfillment of a dream. It was something Chip and I had dreamed and accomplished *together*. From scratch. It wasn't his business that I added to, or my business that he added to. It was *ours*. At some point every day, no matter what he had going on out at the various job sites, Chip had been there with me, sitting in that little back office at the desk right next to the Pack 'n Play, doing his thing while I did mine.

I will remember 'til the day I die the moment I stood on the front steps and locked that shop door for the last time as tears rolled down my face.

Even as I stood on those steps, trying to say good-bye, I kept asking God, "Are you sure this is the right move? If it is, why does it seem so painful and hard?"

That's when I heard that gentle whisper, *Joanna, if you trust me with your dreams, I'll take them further than you could have ever imagined.*

It is no easy thing to trust in God, to walk away from a career, to give it all up not knowing if you can ever get it back or even come close. But I did it. I heeded his voice, and somehow I found peace about it.

We put the shop on the market and hoped to find a buyer for that property as soon as possible. Obviously we wanted to respect it, the way Maebelle had respected it when she sold it to us. We still loved Maebelle, who had become like a grandmother to us. We used to visit her in the nursing home where she lived now and be her guests when they had pancake suppers.

But we just couldn't afford to hold on to the building out of principle, the way she had.

We both would have loved for someone to have saved that old building we'd worked so hard to fix up, but there just wasn't another Chip and Joanna out there who were looking for a property like that one. We couldn't keep paying a mortgage on a shop that wasn't open. So we told ourselves, "It is what it is. We need to move on. We'll see what happens." If someone came along and made us a decent offer, we would just have to cross that bridge when we came to it.

We considered offers from some other developers and business owners and kept trying to make a deal. But for some reason, those deals kept falling through.

What's interesting to me is that just as Jo closed up the shop, Magnolia Homes was starting to rock and roll. At the very same moment we were trying to sell that building, we were also looking for some office space for the company. We needed a place where we could hire a secretary to do the books. But we also needed a spot with some outdoor space where we could store supplies and materials, and possibly have a staging area for "the Boys" to gather what they needed before heading to a particular job site for a day.

I was out driving around with a buddy of mine who'd been helping me look for a good location, and he'd actually found a couple of spots around town, but we had never found a spot that jumped out at me.

We happened to turn down Bosque as we were driving, and he asked me, "What's the deal with the shop? Have you sold it yet?"

I told him we'd hit a few snags and hadn't been able to close a deal. And right as we were driving past it, he said, "Well, have you ever thought about using that for your office?"

It was like a giant lightbulb went on over my head. I swung the truck back around and pulled into the parking lot. I looked at that building with a whole new set of eyes. It had the parking lot in the front, but there was also an area in the back that was plenty big enough for a storage unit that could hold the lumber and materials we kept on hand or anything else we might need to store. It had an office in the back that was ready to go. And why couldn't we turn the front part, where the retail shop had been, into more office space too? The mortgage we were paying on that little building was less than the rent I'd be paying by a pretty good margin.

"Dude, you're a genius!" I said.

The very next day we jumped in and started renovating that store into the Magnolia Homes headquarters, adding the office and storage space that would make it home for our construction company.

Funny that we needed an outsider to bring that to our attention. We had always seen the building as our shop. But now it was "our" headquarters, and we were getting to hold on to that precious building. We could even keep our Magnolia sign.

It felt right. The whole thing felt right. Being at home as a full-time mom meant giving up the shop, but it didn't mean giving up on everything else.

Chip and I started working more closely together than ever. My design ideas were the backbone of Magnolia Homes, and I'd wind up coming in and out of that construction office as often as Chip had been in and out of the back office when it was my store. In the coming months, I'd actually figure out a way to stay in touch with all of my clientele and my wholesalers and to continue Magnolia as a home-furnishings brand without having a physical shop too.

I felt good about having made the decision to walk away and lock that door. It's funny, though, looking back on it now, because one very simple concept in life never occurred to me as I was walking away:

Even locked doors can be unlocked in time.

I simply never could have imagined just how much God had in store for us, and I certainly couldn't have dreamed just how many keys to other doors God had already placed in our hands.

## EIGHT

# DOWN TO OUR ROOTS

For the next four years, Chip and I were dedicated to one thing: raising our beautiful babies.

In addition to Drake and Ella Rose, who was born in October of 2006, our family would come to include two more children, Duke and Emmie, who were born in 2008 and 2010, respectively. But when talking about our "babies," we also mean our business. The reach of Magnolia Homes quickly expanded beyond our little neighborhood on Third Street and into other areas all over Waco.

We had the opportunity to do all sorts of remodeling and renovation projects in a wide variety of homes, including some beautiful old homes in a historic part of town called Castle Heights. We did work there for some of the people who had frequented my now-closed shop—the wives of doctors and lawyers. And then, when they saw what we were capable of doing, those folks spread the word to neighbors and friends who had money to invest in more extensive remodeling projects.

This wasn't just changing throw pillows and paint colors. We put Chip's growing expertise to work and added the capability and muscle the Boys brought to the table to start tearing down walls, installing French doors, and creating new entryways—all catered to our clients' tastes through the filter of my own evolving design aesthetic.

Driving through the Castle Heights neighborhood, I was immediately drawn to it. I think almost anyone would be. It was full of beautiful, stately old homes with well-kept lawns, mostly tucked back off the main roads where there wasn't much traffic, so kids could play and ride bikes in the streets. And it wasn't a snobby sort of place either. Neighbors seemed to know each other, and their kids played together regularly. It seemed out of reach for us, and yet once we started working in those homes, I quickly started to dream about living in that neighborhood.

"*Someday*," I said to Chip.

And, well, you already know how my "somedays" worked out when I spoke them out loud to Chip. But I'll share a little more about that in a bit.

Looking back on those years, the thing that strikes me is that it all seemed to happen so fast. Maybe it was just a lack of sleep from having four kids in quick succession, but those years just seem to blur together for me.

I suppose a lot of young couples feel that way once kids come into the picture. Time does fly, just as those other moms had told me.

Every time I turned around, it seemed as though Drake had suddenly grown another inch or Ella Rose had started walking, or Duke and Emmie were sleeping through the night. These huge milestones came one on top of the other, and I felt truly blessed to be able to work from home so I never missed one—not to mention getting to work alongside my husband as we grew our business together.

The magic that Chip and I had discovered early on—that we seem to grow stronger the more time we spend together—never seemed to wear off. We were well past the honeymoon stage in our marriage, and yet we seemed to fall even more in love with each other now that we had children. We both fell more in love with our work, too, with every new project we tackled as a team.

Don't get me wrong. Juggling that sort of entrepreneurial career with four little kids was not easy. It seemed that no matter how hard we worked, no matter how many extra jobs we picked up, we were still barely scraping by and living with huge amounts of debt. Chip never stopped pulling crazy stunts, and each time I'd get just as angry over them as I'd gotten when he left Drake home alone those two times in his first few months.

But we always worked things out. Always. If we hadn't had each other to lean on, I don't know how we would have gotten through it all.

With two, then three, then four kids in the house, there wasn't very much time to think about the hows and whys of what made our relationship or our business tick. It seemed like everything just kept moving along. Thank goodness we had built our life on a strong foundation.

I think it was more than just the foundation of our own relationship, though. Part of what made Chip and I work so well together was clearly buried down deep in our roots. It came from our families and our upbringings and the challenges we'd already tackled within ourselves before we even met.

I've already mentioned that my early years were spent in Wichita, Kansas. That's where I was born in 1978, the middle of three girls. Teresa, the oldest, and Mary Kay (Mikey), the youngest, are still my closest friends today. But the roots I'm talking about really go back somewhere in the DNA of my parents, two completely unique people who met and fell in love back in 1969.

My dad was drafted to serve in Vietnam that year, when nearly all of the men who were drafted were sent straight to combat. But not my dad. He was held back in his class because of a case of shingles and ended up being sent to Seoul, Korea, six months later than originally planned.

During Dad's first few months overseas, while at a party with his friends, he met my mom for the first time. Though she was taking English classes at the time, she wasn't able to speak much just yet. But she was fascinated by the American culture, which she'd been exposed to from watching American movies. It seemed to her that women weren't treated with the kind of respect in Korea that they were in America. She hoped that by learning the language she'd learn more about the culture as a whole.

Interestingly enough, the way my mother tells it, she spotted my dad sitting off by himself in a corner at that party and said to a friend of hers, "That's the man I'm going to marry." Her friends thought she was crazy, but she says she just knew.

She wound up hanging around my dad and his friends a lot after that night. As it turned out, one of his good friends really liked her, but she always knew my dad was the one. After a few months they finally started dating—just before it was time for Dad to fly home.

Once he was back in America, the two of them began writing letters back and forth to each other. Whenever a new letter arrived, my dad would take it to a translator to have her words read to him, and she would do the same whenever his letters arrived in Seoul.

Everything was going well until my dad sent her an airline ticket and a letter that said, "Will you marry me? Come to America." Then my mother got a case of cold feet. It was what she'd always dreamed about, but it was a life-changing decision for her to make—and she had to make it fast.

Of course, ultimately she came and joined him in America, and he went to the Los Angeles airport to pick her up. They were married by a justice of the peace in Las Vegas in 1972 and then went to live in Wichita, Kansas, my dad's hometown. My dad had been raised Catholic and my mom had been raised Buddhist Korean, so neither set of parents approved of the marriage in the beginning.

From what they've told me, they actually had a rocky marriage for several years. My dad experimented with drugs, as many did back in the seventies, and this behavior was an issue between them. Communicating with one another over a cultural and language divide was surely a challenge as well. There were times, they say, when they didn't think they would make it because all they did was fight.

It wasn't until my father lost his grandmother, shortly before I was born, that he had an awakening of sorts. He was at her house after she'd passed away and was having a pretty bad trip. He envisioned himself in a casket, with his family surrounding him, and it hit him just how wrongly he was living his life. He knew he didn't want to end up in that casket the way he envisioned, leaving my mom alone to fend for herself. So he ran out of his grandmother's house and pleaded to God, "If you let me live, I promise I will turn my life around."

Through this promise, my parents discovered a faith in God from which there was no turning back. The two of them began memorizing Scripture together each day. This practice helped them discover new wisdom, and their marriage found itself on solid footing for the first time, and continued from that point forward.

My dad's father, my grandfather, had worked three jobs to support his big family of kids. By watching him, my dad had picked up a strong work ethic that kicked fully into gear right around the time I was born. That's when he went to work for Firestone, and every promotion after that meant moving our whole family to a new town.

By the time we got to Waco, Dad owned his own Firestone dealership, which was a dream come true for him. By that point my family had lived in seven or eight different houses, from Wichita to Corpus Christi, Texas, to Round Rock, just outside of Austin, Texas. Each one of those moves was a family decision. He sat us all down and discussed it every time, and each time we kind of knew it was coming. We were always sad to leave those places that had become home for us, but we were also always happy for dad and his pursuit of bigger and better opportunities.

Moving was never easy for me, though. This was due in part to my own insecurities, which trace back to my experiences in first or second grade back in Rose Hill, Kansas, when kids started noticing that I didn't look exactly like they did.

As a small child I had never noticed there was anything different about me. I thought I looked like everybody else. And really, most people don't look at me and automatically think I'm half-Korean. But in those first couple of years in elementary school, kids started picking on me because of it.

The worst of it came in the lunchroom. I would get served the same broccoli-and-cheese rice that everyone else in the lunch line was served. But a group of boys—especially this one redheaded boy—would start saying things like "Oh, look at the little Asian girl eating rice." Going to the lunchroom caused me so much anxiety that I asked my mom to start packing me a cold lunch instead. The kids who ate cold lunch gathered in a separate room, where it wound up just being me and a handful of other girls.

I thought I was in the clear then—until my grandmother came to live with us for a while and started attending school events. She looked like a traditional grandmother from South Korea. It was her first time in the United States, she wore no makeup, and all the children seemed to notice how different she looked from the average Kansas grandma. This seemed to give that group of boys more reason to make fun of me.

As a child I didn't know how to process all this. I just felt the pain of being different, and I felt I had to be something else in order to be accepted.

Luckily, kids grow out of that unfiltered phase, and the torment soon just sort of went away. The rest of my elementary school and middle school years were pretty normal. They were fun. Getting picked on for being different wasn't an issue I consciously carried with me as I grew. It wasn't something I worried about. I always made friends, and for years that old fear of walking into the cafeteria stayed buried somewhere deep in my subconscious.

Moving every few years left me feeling like I could never get comfortable, though. Just when I started to settle in somewhere and find my footing, I'd wake up, and it would be time to move again. I learned to just accept it. I trained myself to get used to it. And I suppose that set me up for my life with Chip in a big way. We may not have been making cross-country moves in our marriage, but moving from house to house is still a big change, and we would make a lot of those transitions.

I think the toughest move of all for me as a kid was between Corpus Christi and Round Rock. It happened during my sophomore year of high school. I'd gone to private school most of my life, so I was used to having maybe thirty people in my class. When I moved to Round Rock High School, there were nearly *six hundred* kids in my class. This came as a complete culture shock to me. We also moved in the middle of the year, and that made it even tougher, especially on the first day.

I had always made friends easily on my first day of school. When you're the new girl at a private school, everyone's excited to see a new face. But being the new girl at a large public school in Texas was different. I swear no one even noticed me. I wondered if they even noticed that I was new. For all they knew, I could have been there for years and just blended in.

I walked into the lunchroom on that first day at Round Rock High, and every bad feeling I had felt as a second grader came flooding back. I was literally crippled by it. In my mind I saw myself in a spotlight, a little girl walking into that crowd of people who would surely look at me as different. I was sure they were going to make fun of me.

In reality, I don't think anyone even noticed me, but I still felt awful. I walked through that cafeteria without making eye contact with any-body, went straight into the bathroom, and hid in a stall. I stayed in there for thirty minutes, right up until I heard the bell ring.

I wound up doing that every day for the rest of the semester, from January through May. I spent lunchtime either hiding in the bathroom or ducking into a quiet corner of the library.

I'm not sure why I was so terrified. Maybe it was just teenage hor-mones, but I never even gave those kids a chance to ask me to sit with them. I felt their rejection and acted on it before I even gave them a chance.

At some point my mom realized I wasn't eating lunch. She got mad at me at first. Then she said, "I'm going to pick you up. You have to eat." Sophomores weren't allowed to leave campus at lunchtime, so I had to sneak off campus to jump into my mom's getaway car. Once or twice a week we'd plan it so she'd be there at 11:15 on the dot. I would bolt out and jump over the rope at the edge of the lawn. My mom would have the car door open, waiting for me, and we'd take off. She'd take me to Wendy's and then secretly drop me back at school before the start of the next period. And each time she'd say, "Jo, listen, we can't keep doing this. You've got to make friends."

Mom wasn't enabling my fearful behavior. It was simply her motherly instinct; she wanted her teenage daughter to eat. As a mother now myself, I can't blame her. And now, looking back, those lunches stand out as some of my favorite times with my mother. We were kind of like lunchtime bandits, stealing away for twenty minutes together to laugh and talk and grab a burger together.

Over the course of the summer, I did make a few friends, and by the start of the next school year it all sort of worked itself out. It took me a good six months of awkwardness to finally find a friend group through gymnastics—and then we up and moved again in the middle of my junior year.

I arrived at my small private school in Waco (in a class of twenty-eight people) on the same day a group of Chinese exchange students were visiting the school. Everyone mistakenly thought I was one of them—a Chinese girl who just happened to dress American and didn't have an accent. Everyone was kind of intrigued by that. It served as an icebreaker that gained me some friendships from the get-go.

Right after we moved to Waco was when I started working with my dad at the Firestone dealership and started to get involved both at school and at church. It wasn't until my senior year, though, that I first started to think consciously about what it meant to be half-Korean.

I remember thinking, *I'm either white, Korean, or both, but I've got to own this. It's* me. I started to see how beautiful my mom's culture was and how beautiful she was, and there were times when I wanted people to know she was different and she was unique. I didn't want to be embarrassed about that.

To my surprise, in the fall of my senior year I was actually elected as our high school's homecoming queen. I remember walking out on the football field to be crowned, thinking about how radically different this feeling was from the rejection I'd felt just two years prior, hiding in bathroom stalls at lunchtime. I was thankful my high school career had ended on a good note. I felt there was redemption in my heart from an old wound that had never truly healed.

A few years later I graduated from Baylor University as a communications major, traveled to New York, and finally got rid of the second-grade chip on my shoulder. After all those years of failing to understand or embrace what an honor it was to be a part of my mother's amazing culture, I finally believed it was actually a beautiful thing to be unique and to be different.

And this, of course, was right around the time when Mr. Different-and-Unique himself, Chip Gaines, walked into my life.

# NINE

## CHIPPING IN

As I mentioned earlier, my mom and dad grew up in Archer City, Texas, a town of maybe two thousand people. When compared to Archer City, Waco would have been like the big city where you would come see a movie on the weekend or something.

My parents aren't ashamed to tell anybody that their whole group of friends in that town were all poor growing up, but my dad was the poorest kid of the bunch. He lived in what would be the equivalent of the projects in that town, and the government paid a portion of the rent for the apartment where he grew up.

His mom, my grandma, was a single mom raising two kids back in the day. In a town where everybody was broke, they were known as the poor family. So to my dad, my mom seemed like a rich girl just because her dad was a rancher and they had a house and some cows.

The two of them started dating in the eighth grade, and their small-town romance never let up. In those days, in that town, just a few folks had gone to college; no one's mom had gone to college. Nobody even thought about college, and even if they had wanted to go, no one could have afforded it. College wasn't really an option.

My dad would probably have graduated high school and become a mechanic or something like that. But then he started playing football, and he was good at it. He received a football scholarship to the University of New Mexico, and the whole world opened up to him.

He went off to Albuquerque, and to his small-town mind it was as big of a change as moving to Las Vegas or New York might be to somebody else. I mean, to him it was just the coolest place in the world. He got himself out of Texas for the first time ever and started learning about who he really was. The school was in the Western Athletic Conference (WAC), which played Hawaii, so he got to go to Hawaii. Twice. Before that, he had never even been on a plane!

My mom stayed in Texas and wound up going to a nearby college called Midwestern State. She and Dad carried on a long-distance relationship for two years. Then she transferred to UNM so they could be together—the football star and the cheerleader, the polar opposite of Jo's parents in many ways.

When my dad stayed on as a fifth-year senior, they got married, and my older sister, Shannon, came along shortly thereafter.

My dad was so excited and motivated by sports and athletics that, after he graduated, he opened a sporting goods store there in Albuquerque, the city where I was born in 1974. My parents tell me that even way back then I had a way of making friends with just about everybody, and I always wanted to do things for others. I was always asking my mom for money to give the homeless people we passed on the streets. And whenever some kid would come knocking on the door, trying to sell something, I'd say yes before he even started his pitch—then go running into the back of the house to get the money.

"Why do you need five dollars, Chip?" my parents would ask.

"Because I already bought this thing. This kid needs the money. Please!"

For some reason, even as a kid, I didn't qualify people like most folks do. I treated everybody the same. From a young age I understood the true meaning of the golden rule. I literally treated others as I wanted to be treated.

It probably comes as a surprise to no one that I had a certain wild streak as a kid. I had this great friend named Devon who lived directly across the street from me in our cookie-cutter suburban neighborhood. Our driveways sloped down toward the street, and the two of us would ride our Big Wheels down those hills and shoot directly across the road into each other's driveways, most of the time without looking.

Every other day, someone would have to slam on their brakes and come to a squealing halt to avoid hitting one of us. Then some mom would come knocking on our door and shout at my parents, "He didn't even look! He just scooted out. I almost hit him!"

We never stopped doing it, though. We just kept on zipping across, back and forth, pulling the emergency brake and spinning to a stop right at each other's mailbox. Listen, if the Dukes of Hazzard did it, we attempted it on those Big Wheels.

There was nothing terribly difficult about my childhood—certainly nothing like Jo felt when she walked into the school cafeteria. I always joke that my name was Chip, and that was tough enough. But other than that I was this athletic kid with friends, and I thought I had a pretty good life.

My only problem, if you want to call it a problem, is that I just never fit society's mold, especially at school. I was always talking at inappropriate times. I was always getting in trouble with teachers who said I didn't do things right. I wasn't writing right. I wasn't staying inside the lines. There was always some structure that I just somehow couldn't fit my little brain into. (That probably doesn't come as a surprise to anyone who knows me either.)

I never thought of my dad as an entrepreneur per se. I thought of him more as a businessman. And yet I seemed to pick up the entrepreneurial spirit from somewhere early on. I remember having my mom drive me down to the tennis courts, where I'd sell juice boxes to the kids in summer camp. I obviously wasn't getting rich off of this little business, but it was fun, and it taught me a little about money and work.

My parents did teach me the value of a dollar—and of hard work too. We were always working together as a family, out in the yard or inside the house. That was the beginning of a thought that became a full-fledged goal after I graduated from college. I told myself that I was going to live the rest of my life as if it were Saturday.

I told that to Jo early on, and she was a bit put off by that. At one point she said to me, "Chip, life just isn't like that. Life isn't always Saturday." I realized I needed to clarify what that phrase meant to me—so I suppose I ought to clarify it here too.

When I was growing up, Saturdays weren't always easy for us. In our house, you didn't sleep in until noon and then go to the beach. We would wake up at seven thirty on Saturday mornings and pull weeds until eleven. Once we were all sweating our brains out, then out came the lemonade, or here came the Popsicles. Then it was usually back to work—cleaning the house, cleaning our rooms, maybe helping Dad with some project. But when evening came, we would pack up the car and go for a real treat.

A real treat to us sometimes just meant McDonald's for dinner. If it were a big treat, Mom and Dad would take us camping for the night, or maybe we'd go to a movie once in a while. Whatever it was, it was fun. And that's what Saturday came to mean to me.

For us, Saturdays weren't about work, even though we did a lot of work. They weren't about going to an office somewhere, or to school, and having the whole family separated for the whole day. Saturdays were less structured. They were about getting the work done so you could go jump in the pool or have an ice cream cone.

There was something about school that didn't work for me— something about the fact that you had to turn in these assignments and you had to be there exactly when they said or else there was some disciplinary effort. Even before I got out of college, I vividly remember thinking, *I'm gonna put up with this for as long as I have to. But the second I don't have to put up with it anymore, I'm out. And I'm gonna live every day for the rest of my life as if it's Saturday.*

There would be times in the coming years when I would be flat broke and think, *Maybe I messed up. I feel like I'm living every day as if it's Monday!* But that feeling would never last long. Whenever I've been down financially, I've just picked myself up and worked a little harder. And whether it's a little luck or God or a combination, everything seems to find a way of working itself out eventually.

One thing my dad would preach to us when it came to money was, "I'll provide your needs, but you have to take care of your wants." So once I was old enough, if I told my parents I wanted some new toy or gadget, they'd say, "Well, great. There's this lawn two doors down that we keep driving by and noticing that it needs to be mowed. What if you went and knocked on that guy's door and asked him if you could mow it. How much is this thing you're looking for?"

"Well, it's twelve bucks."

"Okay. Well, if you offered to mow it for five, it would only take you two or three weeks, and you could have it!"

They never said no or "quit asking." They just said, "If you want that thing, here's an idea as to how you can go earn it."

There were times when I chose to be the lazy kid and wouldn't bother. And there were other times when I decided I really wanted something, so I'd grab the lawn mower and head down the street, knocking on doors.

When I was in third grade, my parents moved us to the Dallas area. Dad sold his sporting goods business and wound up landing a good job with American Airlines. It was a real corporate kind of a job, but my dad still managed to put his family first. He'd be home around five-thirty every night, and right after dinner he'd be out in the driveway shooting hoops with my sister, who was into basketball. Sometimes they'd play until nine or ten o'clock at night.

When I got a little older, I really took to baseball, and Dad did the same thing with me. Every night and every weekend, he'd be out there pitching balls to me and teaching me to field grounders.

The thing is, I started to get good at it. Dad got a bit of a gleam in his eye, thinking I might be some kind of a star player. I loved seeing him get so excited about it, and that made me try even harder.

For my dad, achieving goals was basically a mathematical equation: "If you hit a hundred balls a day and you work out this many hours, this many times a week, then this is what happens and you win state championships."

I followed his advice and, lo and behold, A plus B really did equal C for me. If I did this, then I achieved that. I started to become the star player he envisioned. I received all sorts of accolades, and everybody thought I was the greatest thing ever.

In some ways it was easy. It was just this mathematical thing. It would help keep me on the straight and narrow as I got into high school too. When a buddy was going off to a party, I could easily walk away by saying, "Man, I'd love to go and have a few beers—I'm not gonna lie to you. But jeez, I gotta go take a hundred ground balls. If I don't take a hundred ground balls every day, then I don't make the state tournament, and then I don't get a scholarship to go play ball in college."

Being a star athlete in high school sort of automatically buys you a lot of friends and attention. I was always the guy who had funny stories to tell, so when I walked into the cafeteria at Grapevine High School, everybody was calling me to come over to their table and eat with them. I just led a charmed life.

But somehow, instead of taking that and just running with it like some kids do, I never let go of that spirit I had when I was little—that desire to lift people up along with me and help them out if I could. I made friends with a kid who had Down syndrome, grabbing him to come play football with us on a Saturday afternoon. One of my friends was an Asian boy who'd been adopted from Vietnam. I just always loved getting to know people, all kinds, even if they weren't athletes or in the "popular" crowd.

Some of these friends of mine lived in the same neighborhood I did, so naturally we all became close. It was easy to make friends with the kids who lived close by, but I didn't forget about them in the cafeteria or in the hallway just because things were "different" at school. It was just never like that for me. I didn't like being put in a certain box, and I didn't appreciate people doing that to my friends either.

Being a popular guy in school actually had its downside. Sometimes I just wanted a day off. I felt a lot of pressure to show up to friends' parties, and people were let down when I didn't make it or even if I left early. It was actually a lot to live up to.

He's not a bragger, so he won't say these things if I don't speak up here, but Chip was the football captain at the same time he was playing scholarship-worthy baseball in high school. He was also voted "Most Likely to Succeed," "Most Likely to Be the Next President"—whatever you think a charmed-life kid would have, he had it.

I did. That's true. But the pressure of being Mr. Perfect, Mr. All-American, Mr. Most-Liked, and Mr. Well-Dressed was a lot to take, especially since my grades weren't very good. I became sort of addicted to the applause and praise, even from my parents, and I just felt awful anytime I let anybody down. Honestly, when I didn't play so well in a game and I saw the disappointment on my dad's face, it was hard. He had such high hopes for me, and I wanted to live up to them.

In some ways it's as if I was the Zack Morris character in that teen series *Saved by the Bell*. I was that guy. And our school was that wholesome in a lot of ways too. When we got in trouble, it was for TP'ing the vice principal's house or something. It was all "Come on, guys; let's win a state championship" or "Do the right thing."

There were nearly seven hundred people in my graduating class, but there was very little in terms of drugs, at least as far as I was aware. There was plenty of alcohol around, but I was scared to death of getting caught, so I pretty much steered clear. I seemed to have this innate ability to do the right thing and somehow make it look cool simultaneously.

Then I wound up playing baseball at North Lake Junior College, and going to that school was just a complete culture shock. A lot of the kids who went to that school came from very different backgrounds and seemed to have very different worldviews. I was used to being around disciplined athletes who dedicated themselves to being the best they could be on and off the field. But at North Lake some of the best athletes on the team were the rowdiest dudes. Athletes who were much better than I was were doing all sorts of things they shouldn't have been doing at the parties we went to.

Interestingly enough, girls hung around that team almost like groupies, and I hadn't expected that kind of thing at a junior college. It was eye-opening. I felt like I was an innocent *Leave it to Beaver* character from the 1950s watching this wild spectacle from the sidelines. I went on dates with pretty girls, and I hung out at the parties, but I just never got into the whole scene. I never fit in. That was a weird position to be in after feeling like the king of Grapevine High.

I did manage to make friends with a couple of guys who were more like me, and those friendships helped get me through that first year, but my heart just wasn't there. I got this little notebook and started journaling, writing songs, and sketching out business plans in it. I'd spend hours in my apartment writing down my thoughts and ideas in that thing. I'd never done that before, but it was strangely therapeutic. I wish I could actually find that notebook. I would love for Jo to see it since that's so fitting in her personality.

That was the only season in my life when I ever tried to do any of those artsy-type things. I was just trying to express something that needed to come out, I suppose. And I'm sure it was one way of dealing with my loneliness.

I wanted out of that junior college. And luckily enough, a recruiter for Baylor happened to be in the stands when I made one of the greatest plays of my entire baseball career. I was playing second base, and I made this diving grab on a shot hit between first and second base. Then somehow I twisted around as I slid through the dirt to make a monster throw and get the runner out at first.

That recruiter offered to get me into Baylor and to make sure I would have a spot in the athletic dorm. I honestly couldn't even tell you if they covered my books, because I didn't care. I took it. I was ready to leave North Lake and start fresh.

As it turned out, I loved Baylor. I loved being around all those rich kids, even if I was nothing like them. I loved the girls. I loved the campus. I wasn't a very good student, and I struggled to pass every semester. But I did fall in love with the city of Waco and started to see myself staying in that town pretty much forever, especially once I started mowing lawns.

It's funny. Here I was, at this prestigious school, playing baseball and studying business. But instead of daydreaming about the major leagues or running some Fortune 500 company, I found myself in class looking out the window at the guys mowing grass and wishing I could trade places with them.

My junior year at Baylor, I decided that was exactly what I was going to do. I wasn't going to quit school. I would stay and finish my degree in business. But I wanted to go out and make money like I did as a kid—and not just in the summertime, the way I did with the book company and the fireworks stands. I wanted to work while I was going to school, to get outdoors, to start my own business. And I knew I would have to give something up if I was going to find the time to do that.

Turned out, the thing I needed to give up gave up on me first. A new coach came to Baylor and decided he wanted to make some major changes, so I was gone, along with a bunch of other guys who were on partial scholarships. And just like that, everything changed.

My dad was all fired up about my transferring to another school and finding a scholarship, and a few of my baseball buddies would go on to do that with great success. But I wasn't interested in chasing baseball all over the country. I had already seen the writing on the wall. I was a good baseball player, but I wasn't good enough to turn it into a full-time career. It just wasn't meant to be. It was time to move on.

I dreaded telling my dad, though. He'd spent all those years throwing balls to me for hours and hours every day. He'd come to every single one of my games, going all the way back to when I was a little kid, and when I grew older he'd acted almost as my agent or manager when it came to talking to schools or considering my future in the sport. He was so proud of me, and knowing I was going to let him down was pretty hard for me.

I put off that conversation for as long as I could, just worrying and worrying myself to death over how he was going to react. When I finally told him, I had tears in my eyes. But my dad looked at me and said, "Son, I love you. If you're telling me baseball is out, then it's out. It's okay."

It was this beautiful conversation. He was concerned about what I was going to focus on. I was too! My whole life had been about baseball, and when he asked me what I wanted to do, I told him I had no idea.

I told him I wanted to go out and maybe earn some money and start up a little business, and all he said was that whatever I did, he hoped I was as dedicated to it as I'd been to baseball. He wanted me to go out and hit the proverbial hundred balls every day, to give it my all no matter what I was doing.

I just remember vividly, for the first time in my life, really knowing in my heart of hearts that my dad loved me no matter what. It wasn't tied to baseball. It wasn't tied to something I did or didn't do. It was just an awesome feeling to realize that. And to this day that is one of the best conversations I've ever had with my old man.

I think I learned another lesson that day too: Sometimes worrying about something is much worse than the actual thing you're worrying about. So really, what's the point in worrying?

# TEN

# FLIPPING OUT

By the time Chip and I met, he'd managed to combine these two conflicting sides of himself: the kid who steered clear of trouble and did the right thing, and the kid who rode his Big Wheel full speed into the street without looking both ways. I had never met anyone like him. It's funny to me to think that the whole opposites-attract thing might have been programmed into my DNA. Just as my outgoing mother was drawn to my quiet dad, I was this shy girl drawn to the super-outgoing Chip Gaines. And the fact that he owned a successful lawn and irrigation business and had made up his mind that he loved Waco and wanted to stay put was somehow a perfect fit with everything I knew I wanted myself.

Jo didn't even realize that the lawn and irrigation business I was running when we met was actually the third version of that business I had launched. I'd managed to start each of these lawn businesses from scratch, build a clientele, and then sell it lock, stock, and barrel—meaning clientele, equipment, and employees—to somebody else. And that was on top of getting into the business of buying houses as rental properties, plus a little corner wash-and-fold business that I'd started. I almost forgot to mention that.

It all began when I tracked down the owner of the lawn service that took care of Baylor's landscaping. Remember when I'd look out the window and wish I could trade places with the guy mowing the grass? Well, that guy worked for this man. His name was David. And when I asked him for a job, he didn't think twice—he just simply told me no.

David was this real interesting guy who lived in a loft apartment he'd built inside his lawn company's warehouse. You'd never guess by looking at him, but I swear he was worth millions of dollars. I chatted him up the way I chat lots of people up, and I wouldn't take no for an answer. I wanted to get a job cutting grass, to learn the trade from the inside out. So I asked him, "How did you get your start?"

He said, "I don't know. I quit school in the seventh grade and just started mowing grass."

I kept asking questions, and he kept answering. Turns out, he was a really, really smart guy, and he basically became a mentor to me. I grew to call him Uncle David, and it's almost like I was sitting at his feet, as if he were some old guy whittling a stick on a front porch, teaching me these million-dollar life lessons. So I was getting the academic side at Baylor and learning common sense from one of the most commonsense guys on the planet. It was the perfect education for me.

Oh, and he finally hired me. I was persistent, if nothing else. And I grew to love that man, even though he was hard on me. He wasn't a real encouraging guy by nature. As a matter of fact, he used to joke to all his buddies that hiring me "was like losing two of his best guys."

I didn't mind. I had always had thick skin—thick skin and a positive self-image—so it took a lot to shake me. But one day after having worked a few months under Uncle David, I was on campus mowing with his guys, and I saw a fraternity soccer game going on at the intramural fields a few blocks over. Well, like a dog after a squirrel, off I went to watch, leaving my Weed Eater right where it was. Time got away from me, and it got dark before I knew it. My heart dropped when I went back to find the guys all gone—and no sign of the Weed Eater.

That Weed Eater cost what I made in a month, so I knew I was in big trouble. I hitched a ride back to the shop, and with my tail between my legs I told him what had happened. He was upset, but more in an "I trusted you" kind of way. You know, like when your parents would tell you they were disappointed in you rather than yelling. It's almost worse.

David made it clear that if I ever did something like that again, I was gone, and I promised it wouldn't. Right then and there I grew up a little. I realized having fun was one thing, but jacking around on someone else's dime and being flat-out disrespectful was another. I promised myself I'd never disrespect someone that way again.

I must've done all right after that, because Uncle David and I rocked and rolled together for a whole year after that without a hitch. Then one day he said to me, "Son, you're smart. You're going to Baylor University. What are you doing working for me? Go start your own lawn business. You've already seen what we do. Go do it."

He sent me to an equipment company in town, and I priced everything out, and the total for what I needed to get started came to $5,000. I didn't have $5,000. They told me to go across the street to the bank and try to get a loan. So I crossed the street and met a banker named Carroll Fitzgerald.

I had learned a few basic things about putting together a business plan at Baylor, but I didn't think that was enough to get me a loan with no collateral or experience. Carroll didn't think so either. He quickly said no.

But I wouldn't let up. I was a perpetual salesperson. I talked Carroll's ear off, saying, "Look, I've got five lawns I can start tomorrow. That means I'll be making X amount of dollars. I'm gonna quadruple that in a few months, and you guys are gonna make every cent back plus our agreed-on interest. I promise."

Carroll finally gave in and lent me the money—my first $5,000 loan. I walked out of the bank, walked back across the street to the equipment company, and spent every last penny on the things I would need to get my business off the ground in a first-rate way.

I repaid that loan in six months.

I was so excited by the whole thing. I got hooked—hooked on starting businesses, hooked on borrowing money, all of it. I still joke with Carroll to this day that he created a monster. I love borrowing money!

That was my senior year of college. And over the course of the next few years, as I've said, I sold that business off more than once. I built it up to more than a hundred accounts, with a crew, equipment, and a truck. And then I sold it to somebody else who wanted to get into the business.

To be honest, I never made a ton of money off of it. I treated it more like a part-time thing, and I had a lot of expenses paying the crew and everything. But I basically flipped that business the way I'd later start flipping houses. There wasn't always a ton of profit, but it was enough to keep you in the game until you could hit a lick and do it all over again. I was well on my way to building it up and getting ready to sell it again right when I met Jo.

Chip had basically gone through this whole education in the real world of entrepreneurship, and he told me all of these stories as we were first dating. I was in awe. I'd never met anyone who was such a go-getter at such a young age or who did things in such an unconventional way. It was like every time he opened a door, he encountered another door, and another, and he just kept opening every door. In fact, it was his Uncle David who sold him the eleven-acre property on Third Street that would eventually allow us to launch Magnolia Homes.

CHIP ON HIS FAMOUS
BIG WHEEL. THE
SAME ONE THAT
ALMOST CAUSED A
TRAFFIC ACCIDENT.

LITTLE LEAGUE PHOTO
EARLY IN CHIP'S
BASEBALL CAREER.

SCHOOL PHOTO,
SPORTING HIS TURNED-
UP COLLAR.

CHIP HAS BEEN A COWBOY
FROM THE VERY BEGINNING.

CHIP'S FIRST BROKEN BONE . . .
AND IT WOULDN'T BE HIS LAST.

ME AS A BABY
TRYING TO KEEP
WARM IN KANSAS.

THIS IS THE RESULT
OF SCHEDULING
RECESS BEFORE
SCHOOL PHOTOS.

SHOWING OFF MY NEW
HAIRCUT. DON'T THINK
MY HAIR HAS BEEN
THIS SHORT SINCE!

4TH GRADE TRIP TO THE ZOO.

ME AND BOTH OF MY SISTERS—
TERESA AND MARY KAY.

CHIP GOOFING OFF WITH HIS HIGH SCHOOL BASEBALL BUDDIES.

APPEARING IN MY DAD'S FIRESTONE COMMERCIAL, 1996.

A CLASSIC GAINES FAMILY PHOTO!

HIGH SCHOOL GRADUATION WITH MY PARENTS IN 1996.

CHIP'S BAYLOR GRADUATION WITH HIS PARENTS.

EARLY DATING—
THE FIRST TIME CHIP
TOOK ME OUT TO
HIS GRANDFATHER'S
RANCH.

OUR 2002
ENGAGEMENT AT
BILLY HOLDER'S
RING SHOP, ARCHER
CITY, TEXAS.

OUR WEDDING
WAS AT THE EARLE
HARRISON HOUSE—
A HISTORIC MANSION
IN THE WACO AREA.

ONE OF MY FAVORITE
PHOTOS FROM
OUR BIG DAY!

A SHOT FROM OUR
HONEYMOON—
CANOEING IN
NEW ENGLAND.

THE THREE BANDITS
RESPONSIBLE FOR
LANDING CHIP IN JAIL.

FIRST OFFICIAL
DINNER IN OUR VERY
FIRST HOUSE! (AFTER
RENOVATIONS!)

THE SECOND
HOUSE WE FIXED
UP TOGETHER.

CHIP WORKING ON
FENCING AT OUR
SECOND HOUSE.

BRINGING HOME
NEW BABY DRAKE.

THE BOSQUE SHOP
RIGHT AFTER WE
PURCHASED IT . . .

. . . AND AFTER AS
MAGNOLIA MARKET.

OPENING DAY AT
THE ORIGINAL LITTLE
SHOP ON BOSQUE.

INSIDE MAGNOLIA
MARKET WITH OUR
"SHOP BABY" DRAKE!

HOUSE THREE UNDER
CONSTRUCTION!

LITTLE ELLA ALMOST THREE YEARS OLD! PREGNANT WITH EMMIE KAY.

PHOTO TAKEN NOT TOO LONG BEFORE *FIXER UPPER* TOOK OFF!

MY KIDS' PLAYROOM IN THE "SHOTGUN" HOUSE. PHOTO WAS FEATURED ON DESIGNMOM.COM.

THE FIRST GARDEN WE EVER PLANTED TOGETHER.

SHOOTING OUR PILOT EPISODE IN 2012.

FAMILY PHOTO IN THE "SHOTGUN" HOUSE!

HERE'S THE PRE-RENOVATION FARMHOUSE. CAN YOU SEE WHY WE FELL IN LOVE?

FARMHOUSE DURING RENOVATIONS.

THIS IS THE GARDEN CHIP SURPRISED ME WITH AT THE FARMHOUSE!

ONE OF MY FAVORITE ANNIVERSARIES—CHIP SURPRISED ME WITH A 12TH ANNIVERSARY BRUNCH!

That's right. So, my dad had worked his way up the ladder at American Airlines to become a vice president. He was making a good middle-class living. But right around the time I was starting my first lawn business, which would have been 1996 or 1997, he got a call from a corporate headhunter. The guy said, "Hey, we want to recruit you to come over and be the CEO of this office supply products company here in Dallas." He went through the whole interview process, and they wound up offering him the job making five times the money he'd been making at American Airlines.

My parents didn't move into a bigger house or buy fancy cars when they came into that money. They were just never like that. Dad didn't do anything with the extra money except stick it in the bank for a rainy day.

Well, he wound up paying as much in taxes that first year as he'd made the year prior to that, so he quickly got passionate about finding ways to save on taxes. He got some advice from an accountant, and the accountant suggested they should divert some of their income by investing in some properties and businesses.

Dad knew I was always talking up these business ideas. So he asked me if maybe I could help him find a house to invest in around Baylor—something we'd be able to rent out. The very next day, I went and talked to ten people and found him a house.

He ended up buying this little ranch on a couple of acres a few miles from campus for a decent price. He didn't want to manage the renting of it, so he offered me a little bit of money to manage the place for him. I moved into that house with a couple of roommates. They paid rent, which more than took care of the mortgage, and they also helped me fix the place up. We painted it, put in new carpets, all kinds of stuff. And we just had a blast in that little house.

I loved the whole process of helping Dad buy that place, so I kept calling him. "Hey, Dad, I found this other one. Are you interested?"

"Well, hold on," he kept saying. "Let's don't get too crazy. I've already got this one. Obviously, we'll see how it goes. But just hang tight."

A year or so went by, and once my buddies all moved out, Dad and I decided to sell the house. I remember he made probably thirty-five or forty grand on that one house. I was real happy for him, but I also got to thinking that buying and selling houses was a pretty good business to be in.

On top of that, my parents came down and took me out to dinner one night. "You know what?" they said. "We thought about it, and you did a lot of the work that helped us make that profit, so here's a check for a certain percentage of that." They gave me a few thousand dollars, and that got me even more pumped up about the whole house-flipping idea.

Now, flipping houses wasn't exactly a "thing" yet, so people thought I was crazy when I told them that's what I wanted to do for a living. But the wheels in my head just kept turning and turning, and I was determined to find a way to make this work.

I knew my "Uncle David" owned a big eleven-acre tract of land on Third Street with a couple of old, rundown rental houses on it. So I asked him if he'd be interested in selling. He wasn't doing much with that property, and the houses weren't in great shape at that point, so he agreed. My dad and I went in together on that second deal since I had built up a little bit of cash from the lawn-mowing business. We bought that eleven-acre tract for around $110,000. That was certainly a lot of money, but we knew David was giving us a good deal. To this day I'm still thankful to him for that opportunity.

Dad and I also went in together on buying a little commercial plaza right on the edge of the Baylor campus. We rented one corner out to a sandwich shop, and I opened the little wash-and-fold business on the other corner.

That was basically the last thing the two of us went in on together, because once I was a cosigner on those loans with him, the bank that had given him the mortgage on those properties was perfectly willing to loan me money on my own. That's when I got started on my whole "Mayor of Third Street" endeavor. I realized I could make as much money flipping a house as I made running the lawn-care business for a whole year.

So when I met Jo, as she said, I had already been through this whole education—half-formal and half-street. I was ready to keep this entrepreneurial life rolling, and it was after she closed the door to her shop that it all started to click for us. There was something just fantastic about what she and I did together that was far bigger than what either of us was capable of doing on our own.

I wasn't the secret ingredient. I knew how to work hard and how to find good deals, but when we worked together on Magnolia Homes, it was Jo coming in at the end and putting her finishing touch on everything that made all the difference in the world. She was what was so special about our company.

Selling off the bulk of that eleven acres gave us a pretty good windfall just before she closed the shop. We invested that money in some more land and sank it into a few more of the smaller flip houses we were used to doing. We got started building a house from scratch too—our first real "spec home" featuring all of Jo's design ideas that she'd gathered from running her shop and working with her clientele. People loved it.

Then Jo mentioned to me that she'd like to live in a place like Castle Heights someday, and I figured, "Well, maybe we could get into one of those houses that's a bit of a fixer-upper. We could live there and renovate it and flip it for a much higher profit than we do these little student-housing-type homes." It sounded like a bigger risk going in, but I was confident we'd be able to get a bigger return on the back end, so it really wasn't any more of a risk than what we were doing with the smaller homes. I worked out the numbers in my head and said, "Why not?"

I truly thought it would take years of savings and discipline for us to get into a house in that neighborhood. But just a few months after I closed the shop, Chip stumbled onto an opportunity to pick up a gorgeous 1920s Tudor-style house in Castle Heights. The interior was outdated, and the exterior had been neglected. The curb appeal just wasn't there. We'd been living in such small homes that to us the place looked like a mansion. But to people used to living in nicer, bigger houses, it looked like a nightmare. So the owners had priced it right. Thankfully, we had enough cash for a down payment, and at that point we had the credit it would take to make the house ours.

With four babies, we figured it wasn't a great idea to live in a house and renovate it at the same time. So we did the renovations on that Castle Heights home quickly, before we moved into it—and the impression we made was instant. The neighbors couldn't believe how good the exterior looked after just a couple of months.

All we did was paint the exterior and rework the landscaping, but it drew all sorts of attention. Apparently nobody had thought to apply the same sort of fast-moving, flipping-a-house-style renovation ethic to homes in that neighborhood. We did things right. We did quality work. We just did things quickly because that's what we were used to doing.

When you're flipping homes, there are seasons to it. There are times of the year when things sell and times of the year when they don't, and so you get into this schedule of working overtime so you won't lose your shot at making any money. The longer you hold something, the more the interest on the loan will eat into your profit.

Jo and I used to make little bets with each other about how fast we could work. She would say, "You did the floors in two days on that last house. I bet you can do it in one this time!" I'd stay up sanding until two in the morning just to make the bet—and argue that it still counted as the same day.

At the same time that we were renovating the Castle Heights house, things were kind of picking up everywhere for Magnolia Homes. We built our first houses in town, and people were in line to come to our open houses. People were just so taken with Jo's designs that they would come to the open houses even when they had no interest in buying a house. They just wanted to talk to us. "We've got this kitchen, and man, it needs some help. We don't know what to do. Is there any chance we can get you to do our remodel?" We would leave open houses and walk down the block to meet with people who were almost begging us to come do work for them.

It all happened quickly. We seemed to unleash some sort of lightning in a bottle when we started working this deal together.

I was able to do 90 percent of that work from home too. I would hire a babysitter and go out to see a property or check on a job site for a couple of hours here or there in any given week. But I could do all of the actual designing without leaving my kids by using photographs of the location and a sketch pad—and eventually incorporating some design software that I taught myself how to use on the computer. The fact that I was all of a sudden able to do that work from a thirty-six-hundred-square-foot dream home in Castle Heights just seemed beyond imagination. I was in heaven!

Nearly every house in that neighborhood was like a one-of-a-kind work of art. There were homes with grand pillars next to more modern, midcentury homes next to Tudor-style homes next to bungalows built in the twenties and thirties. Just looking out from our new front porch provided me with all sorts of inspiration. And inside our home, I let my inspiration run wild.

I poured everything I had learned up to that point into that house. I had taken to looking at all sorts of architecture and home magazines, and I wanted my home to be worthy of that kind of attention.

So much of what made that house special, however, had nothing to do with what I could do to it. In fact, the best thing I could do for it was to let its character and history come back to life. The reality is that old houses that were built a hundred years ago were built by actual crafts-men, people who were the best in the world at what they did. The little nuances in the woodwork, the framing of the doors, the built-in nooks, the windows—all had been done by smart, talented people, and I quickly found that uncovering those details and all of that character made the house more inviting and more attractive and more alive.

A lot of modern houses in the suburbs are big and beautiful, and I don't want to run anyone down, but when you look closely, it's almost like a beautiful woman with a little too much makeup on. Our Castle Heights home seemed to just get more and more beautiful the more Jo wiped the makeup away.

Mixing the old and the new, bringing our own sense of history into the home—that became really important to me. I think there's some-thing about things from the past that just calls to us, that triggers a kind of longing. Sometimes you look at a piece of furniture or an old clock or a piece of artwork—whatever it might be—and you're just drawn to it. You think, *Why do I love that piece?* Well, chances are it's because it reminds you of something—something from history, something from childhood, maybe even something you lost. This can be true whether the piece is extremely unique and one-of-a-kind or just plain classic.

Take subway tile, for example. Subway tile is the most basic, affordable product in the world. It's not a high-end type of material. But you go into any bakery that ever inspired you—maybe one in France—or you look behind the counters in some cool old restaurant, and what do you see on the walls? Subway tile. You look at old pictures of the New York subway system or delis and coffee shops from a hundred years ago that just draw your eye and make you long for a simpler time, and there it is.

Putting those tiles in a home just works for me. They'll never go out of style. They'll never seem dated. And the more time I spent in that old house in Castle Heights, the more that notion sank into my heart and showed itself in my work.

It's funny how people will get caught up in trends. It's almost like the shag carpet thing in the seventies. People who put it in their houses weren't thinking, *Hey, let's go be dumb.* They were thinking, *This is great. It's gorgeous!* But there are just a lot of trends that come and go, and what Jo was aiming us toward was setting a standard that's the complete opposite of trendy.

Why would I want to encourage my client to use the new hot color when I know that in a year or two she'll need to paint the walls again just to get rid of it? I wouldn't want to do that in my own home. I wouldn't want to waste all that time and money.

I suppose we could have gone in the other direction. I mean, we're businesspeople, right? Why wouldn't we convince the customer to do the hot new color? Then we'd be back every year or two going, "Oh, you're not still doing that orange we talked about last year, are you? That's so outdated. Here, we can give you the newest green for $10,000."

That's just not who we are. And honestly, I'm a creature of habit. I've done my makeup the same way since I was thirteen, and I've always had long hair. I think I've just always liked classic. The Castle Heights house sort of focused me in on it more in terms of design, but in personality I was always that way. I find something I like and I stick with it. Ironically, that's how Chip is too. He's worn the same brand of boots since we married, the same brand of jeans since we married, the same old basic white shirt since we married.

So going after classic, long-lasting looks just made sense to me. My knack for finding antiques and interesting pieces at markets and garage sales certainly didn't die when I closed the shop down. I kept it up in the interest of staging our flip homes and open houses, and I kept many of the most interesting pieces I found for us.

I started to get more creative in how to display my finds too. Building upon the idea that three-dimensional objects add character when they are hung on walls—an idea that started with the fencing window treatment I used in Drake's first nursery—I started hanging baskets on the walls, and then baskets with plates in them. I hung antique gates up to add texture, along with interesting pieces of wood, branches, and other things you might not normally expect to see on a wall.

I started making trips to Canton, Texas, which holds a famous open-air flea market every month called First Monday Trade Days. There I found lots of old, authentic pieces from all over. I frequented the twice-a-year trade days in Round Top, Texas too. And as I did so, I realized my design aesthetic was evolving.

I stopped looking at all the scratches and the scrapes on the old pieces of furniture as flaws. I loved that they told the story of a family that had once eaten at that dining room table—or whatever the story might be. So instead of thinking about how I could refurbish these pieces, I focused on how I could highlight their imperfections. Like houses, the pieces with the best bones were the most fun to bring back to life and the most profitable when I got done.

Some of my early decorating jobs featured all sorts of brand-new pieces of furniture and décor. But I quickly learned that it was the old pieces, the quirky pieces, and the classic pieces that people talked about.

The quirky piece of cabinetry with all sorts of little nooks in it that came from an old hardware store, with notches on the side and little pencil markings where someone used to keep various size bolts organized—I put that piece in my home, and no matter who happens to see it, they'll wind up touching it or saying something or asking questions about it.

There's a life to these old things, and I started to buy more and more of them just to rotate them in the house and play around with how they fit in different settings.

In fact, I was buying so much that I decided to try something new. The one thing I missed most when I started working from home was the interaction with all of my shop clientele, so I thought, *Why not open up a shop right here at home?* Instead of having a store that kept me busy sixty hours a week, I gathered inventory as I went along and decided to open up my house for a Magnolia trunk show three times a year. I filled four rooms of our home with all sorts of finds and displayed them with the same attention to detail I'd paid to the interior design of my shop. Then I invited all my old clients—and all our new neighbors—to come by.

Those trunk shows were more successful than I ever could have imagined. Not only did I sell a lot of product and make some good money, but the neighbors and their friends all had a chance to see what I'd done to the interior of our Castle Heights home. Suddenly all of these folks with really nice homes started asking us to remodel their homes. In about a year's time, with four babies and no advertising or marketing budget whatsoever, we made the jump from renovating eight-hundred-square-foot student-rental houses on Third Street to remodeling some of the finest homes in Waco.

By this time our own home in Castle Heights had been featured in some regional magazines. All that attention meant I started putting pressure on myself to always have my home look clean and put together. But with my older children now toddling around, I found it became harder and harder to maintain both a showroom of a home and a practical space for my family.

One afternoon about four years into this new routine of working from home and making a name for Magnolia Homes, I collapsed onto the couch in a state of complete exhaustion. I only had an hour at most before at least one of the kids woke up from his or her nap. I stared at their toys strewn all over the floor and under the end table, and it stressed me out that I had to pick all that up yet again.

And that's when I first realized that something wasn't right.

I thought about how often I found myself frustrated when the kids would play in the formal living and dining areas. There I was on my couch, in my "beautiful" house, knowing that our business was growing like crazy and I had everything in the world to be thankful for—yet feeling like a total failure.

I looked around and saw a lot of "perfection," and I thought, *But where do my kids sit? Why don't the kids have a play space of their own anywhere in this house?*

Suddenly it hit me like a ton of bricks. In my nonstop efforts to make the house look good and to raise our baby of a business, I had failed to create a space where my children could thrive and be kids. I had neglected to create a home that my most important babies could love too.

# ELEVEN

# HOME-LESS

"JoJo, you awake?"

Of course I wasn't awake. It was midnight. Chip had awakened me from a sound sleep. "What is it?"

"A neighbor called. There's a homeless guy on their front porch, and they aren't sure what to do. I'll be right back."

Even though I was only half-awake and he had caught me completely off guard, there was no way I was leaving this to chance, so as he left the room, I called after him: *Do not bring him home with you!*

I wasn't sure what I was going to do, but off I went. And that night, on a neighbor's front porch, I was introduced to Cedric, a guy who had made a lot of bad choices in his life but who had come to the end of his rope.

I knew Jo wasn't about to have Cedric come sleep on our couch with four babies asleep inside. And I could tell our neighbors needed him to leave as well. So I came up with the only plan I could think of. At one o'clock in the morning, we went to the store and I bought a few blankets and towels, and I took him to a flip house we were about to put on the market. The next day when I went back to check on him, Cedric was still there.

We needed to get that house into final shape for an open house, so Chip offered to put Cedric up in a hotel for a few days in exchange for his doing some work for us. Cedric said yes. He was so grateful for the shelter we had given him that he got out there and worked his tail off for us. It's as if all it took was one chance for him to discover his own work ethic. He started attending a Bible study after that and received services from the Mercy House, a halfway house of sorts that helps people with problems get back on their feet. Come to find out, Cedric had just gotten out of jail, and here he was turning his life around thanks in part to our tiny little bit of help. It was awesome to witness.

As difficult as it was sometimes to put up with Chip's out-of-the-blue surprises, the size of that man's heart brought tears to my eyes. Whether it was a homeless man in the middle of the night, the troubled kids who went to school on Third Street, or neighborhood kids by the shop on Bosque Boulevard, Chip somehow managed to notice them and touch their lives. He became a mentor and father figure to so many people.

Sometimes his kindness and generosity scared me to death, of course—especially when he would stop to pick up a hitchhiker or help someone whose car had broken down on the side of the highway. And I really did push him to do less of that after we had children. But that's just Chip. He can't seem to help it. He's always looking out for someone who looks like they need a break or a helping hand.

He has been modeling those same ideals to our children from the time they were born, and to watch him teach them to value people, to look them in the eye and say "Thank you" and "Hello," is wonderful for me. Chip just automatically does these sorts of basic things that a lot of us overlook and don't realize make a difference.

When I was in my twenties, I thought I'd grow up to be the most liberal parent in the world, but I've actually turned out to be pretty strict and old-fashioned. I'm teaching the kids to always say, "Yes, sir" and "No, sir," and I don't want them playing video games or sitting around doing nothing all day.

I'm right there with him. If these kids want to play, I want them to use their minds and their hands and to go outside.

It's funny how Chip can be so liberal on one hand and so conservative on the other, though. He really is unpredictable. I saw it from the very beginning, and I learned again and again that I simply could not put this man in a box. Just as soon as I would get in the rhythm of some preconceived expectation I thought he fit into, he would turn on a dime and do something completely unpredictable. Then I would have to readjust and recalculate until I finally realized there are just no stereotypes that fit Chip Gaines.

It wasn't too long after our adventure with Cedric that Chip came home with an even bigger surprise: he'd found a couple who wanted to buy our Castle Heights house, so he'd gone out and bought us a new house to move into and flip.

"What?" I said. "Chip, I love this house."

"You were just saying this house isn't good for the kids."

"I know, but we can change that. I mean, Chip—this isn't just another house. This is a *forever* house."

"Jo, this was never meant to be our forever house. We're not ready for our forever house. This isn't everything for us. It isn't everything we want. This is a flip house. It's a *big* flip house. It's a *nice* flip house. But it's still a *flip* house. We knew that going into it."

When Chip drove me over to see the new house, I didn't say a word in the car. I was mentally and emotionally preparing myself so I wouldn't lose it. It was a long, gray, one-story, shotgun of a house that had been built in the go-go-blandness of the 1980s. It had no character. It had no charm. It had no style. It was in a great little pocket neighborhood called Carriage Square, but it sat on a smaller lot than the rest of the houses there, and it backed right up to another family's chain-link fence without so much as a sliver of a backyard. It had a tiny little sloping front yard, too, that ran right into the street. Nothing stately. Nothing old. Nothing beautiful.

I hated it.

Of course, you have to remember that Jo pretty much hated every new flip house we moved into when she first laid eyes on it. I think this one just stung a lot more because we were coming from such a gorgeous old home.

Maybe we had stayed there a little too long. It had been years by the time this all unfolded. We were getting comfortable in that house. And I've gotta say, I don't like it when things get too comfortable.

To me, it's a motivation thing. Comfort is what you do when you retire, so if there's any way you can keep pushing off that "I'm completely comfortable" idea, then it keeps you a little wily; it keeps you young; it keeps you hungry.

It's kind of Rocky-esque. In those movies, Rocky Balboa had all the hunger and desire when he was starting out. It wasn't until after he had the money and the car and the house and the wife and the kid and the dog that something happened and he lost that fire.

For me, I've always thought of moving as a part of that motivation. Houses to me are just investments—inventory, if you will. That's it. So if we've got the money to live in the house that we're in, well then, great. But whenever things get tight, then it immediately comes back to "Hey, this is just an investment." It's like the car dealer who drives the BMW for a couple of weeks knowing if all hell breaks loose, he'll sell the car. Because, again, it's just inventory.

Once we settled into the Castle Heights house, I think we both started to settle into a groove. The business was rocking and rolling, and so we started to think, *We've made it. We're here. Let's just put everything on autopilot.*

But here's something I've noticed. Whenever you do that, whenever you're all settled in and think that's it—that's when the big blow comes that knocks you back down to square one.

That hadn't happened . . . yet. In fact, Waco was pretty steady. We didn't experience the tsunami of economic slowdown that the rest of the country experienced after the housing market collapse in 2008. As we rolled into 2010 and even 2011, the effects of that were just starting to make their way into the Waco economy.

Even that didn't affect us personally, not right off the bat. But I could already see that it was taking us a little longer to move flip properties. Rental income dropped a little bit too. It was just these little incremental things. I wanted to make sure we hedged against that, and the best way I knew how to do that was to sell our current house, take that equity, and downsize a bit. Then we could coast a while if our new home sales or our flip properties took a little longer to sell.

There was another motivating factor to move quickly, too, on top of the fact that I just thought it was time to break out of our comfort cycle and maybe kick our lives into second gear again. In early 2011, we started up a big new investment project. We'd decided to go ahead and develop a tract of land not far from that new shotgun house. It was land that we'd invested in with some of the money we'd made back when my dad and I sold most of our eleven acres on Third Street.

The reason my dad and I had never developed the eleven acres ourselves was that we had lacked the basic knowledge we needed to get it done. Back then we'd been guessing at everything, figuring out where to put streets and curbs and how to get permits.

At one point we thought we could put forty houses on that land. And that was important, because there's tremendous economy of scale when you do a project that big. You can buy all of your lumber and concrete and everything in bulk, which lifts your profit margins in a big way. But we couldn't make the forty houses work. We found out that the bank was only going to lend us enough money to build eight units. Eight! That just wasn't enough.

So we kept messing around with it, and the most we could get financing for was twelve units. That still didn't make economic sense. So we sold the land on Third Street, keeping a little bit of it by the road to put our twelve houses on. And the big developers we sold the land to, who actually knew what they were doing and had the financing, came in and put more than fifty units of student housing on that back parcel of property alone.

We'd struggled to figure out how to get forty units on the entire tract, including the front piece that we'd ended up keeping. They were just better at it than we were, and I learned a ton just by watching that project come together. I knew they were going to make millions of dollars on that deal. So as excited as I was to make hundreds of thousands, I promised myself that one day I'd be doing deals like theirs.

Now, all those years later, I was smarter than I'd been back then. I had more pull with the banks, I had a bigger crew, and I knew people who could draw up the plans and help get the permits through the city. So we got that whole process started, and I knew that it was going to take a lot of money up front to get it done.

That just served as yet another incentive for us to move into the Carriage Square house. Living in that smaller place would cut our mortgage payment in half.

I didn't even like the looks of that house as an investment property, let alone a place to continue raising our family. Yet because of the way Chip does business, I quickly came to the conclusion that—once again— there was no fighting this decision. It was already a done deal. A great couple already had their hearts set on our Castle Heights home, and Chip had already sunk the down payment into that shotgun house at Carriage Square.

By this point, I had learned to adjust my thinking quickly since I never knew what Chip would come up with next. I wanted to stay comfortable, but I finally started to realize that with change comes new opportunity. Even though I was sad to leave our home, I quickly got on board with Chip and thought of all the new memories our family could make in a new place. There was a part of me that was challenged to create beauty in a house that seemed to have no potential.

Once again, we didn't want to do renovations while we were living in a house with four little kids, so we set about doing the renovations just as quickly as we possibly could, before we had to leave that Tudor dream house behind in the rearview mirror.

The guilt I felt over not creating any space in the Castle Heights house where my kids could be themselves was still hanging over me when all of this unfolded, and I made myself a promise that I would make a special place for them in this new house. I think that was my first ever truly intentional design goal: I wanted to make this next house be much more enjoyable and accessible and comfortable for our family. And the more I thought about it, the more I wanted to be intentional about giving each one of us our own things to love about this new house—even if I didn't love the house itself.

*So how will I go about doing that?* I wondered.

I was getting more and more confident about my eye for detail, my ability to find great furniture and objects at flea markets and yard sales and to let the character of those old finds shine through in a way that made any room more interesting. But I'd been applying most of that vision to other people's houses through our renovation and flip projects. I'd even applied it to how people would view our own home—what might look good in a magazine shoot, what people might want to buy when they came to a Magnolia home show, and what might inspire them to hire us to come tackle a renovation project in their home.

As we prepared to make that transition to a smaller house, with a much smaller yard and only one story of living space, I decided to focus in on us. How could I remodel this house to make it work for us?

I would still adhere to the things I'd learned about classic color schemes and using lots of wood and putting three-dimensional objects on the walls, even using pieces that were traditionally for the outdoors. All of those things that appealed to other people were also what appealed to me, so I wasn't ruling anything out or purposefully thinking about making it unattractive to anyone else. I just wanted to put us first. All of us.

I started thinking a whole lot about another mentor of Chip's, Uncle Ricky, the attorney uncle of his college friend—the one who had helped him set up the fireworks-stand business over a couple of summers. What Uncle Ricky did was create this wonderful home environment for his family. He built a beautiful house that was brand-new but looked like it was a hundred years old, and his stunning backyard made you feel as if you were stepping into a vacation somewhere far from Texas the moment you walked out onto their screened-in back porch.

He built up that backyard over many years, adding a cute little setting here and then another cute setting over there, incorporating all sorts of antiques they purchased over the years. I always loved to go there because there was always some new, interesting treasure to see in that backyard.

I don't know if Ricky or his wife have any idea how inspiring that was to me. It wasn't on public display or anything. Nobody but their close friends and family knew any of that stuff was there. It was just for them. But whatever they did, they did it well. And if they couldn't do it all at once, they just built it up over time. They even named the place Teaberry Farm. Ricky had a hat made up with "Teaberry Farm" right on it, and he wore that hat pretty much every single day.

Ricky also kept a bunch of animals back there. They had chickens and goats, and he was always messing around doing something on his tractor. That part of it was a real inspiration to me. He just made life look fun. All those animals and all of those antiques were just a hobby to him. He made his money as an attorney. But he put that money to work in a way that made me want to get to a place like that one day.

All of that was on my mind as I took the kids over to that ugly shotgun house one day to start sketching out some decorating and remodeling ideas. I knew that I didn't have a backyard to work with and less square footage than the Castle Heights house, but I was determined to be creative and to try.

The front door of that house was on one end, by the driveway and garage, and the house just shot back from there in this long, straight, narrow rectangle, with a hallway that ran the length of the house, all the way to the back door by the garage and driveway. Well, no sooner did I open the door than the kids took off down that hall. They started giggling and squealing, and then one of them slipped and kind of fell.

I was worried for a second that somebody had hurt themselves and the whole day would get off on the wrong foot. But that slip and fall made them notice that the floor was slippery to slide on, so all of a sudden the shoes came off and they were running back down this hallway in their socks and sliding straight into the kitchen. You'd have thought we just told them they were going to Disney World, they were so excited. I hadn't done a thing to that house yet, and already my kids were having a better time in it than I'd ever seen them have in my big, beautiful house in Castle Heights.

I went into the house that day thinking I'd try to envision some paint colors and pick who would be in which bedroom. Instead, a lightbulb went on that started to change absolutely everything for me: "My kids love it in here. They can be kids. I'm going to design around that."

Now I wasn't just thinking about making sure the kids had a space they could love. I realized I needed to create a whole house that they could love and I could love and Chip could love. The whole place needed to be practical and functional for them so they could have fun and be themselves in their own home—and we could too.

There were two living rooms in that house, and right then and there I decided to make one whole living room just for the kids. I had this idea to fill bookcases with all of their books, and that got me thinking about what would make Chip happy and what would make *me* happy.

I'd have my kitchen, sure. That was my domain. I was becoming a better cook and really starting to enjoy it. But what would make that even better would be to have a garden so we could have fresh tomatoes and cucumbers and carrots to use. And how much fun would it be to work in the garden with the kids and teach them where their food comes from?

I bolted down the hallway and slid in my socks to the back door with the kids all following right behind me. Then we all went outside and looked. I realized there was just enough land on the side of the house to fence in and turn into a garden. There was even room for a pergola and a little outdoor eating area.

That night I told Chip all about my plans, both inside and out, and he got excited about the outside fenced-in area too. He said, "Can we get some chickens? I've always wanted chickens, like my grandfather had on his ranch."

My response: "Why not?"

That day in that house with our kids was another turning point for me as a designer and a mom. I came to a brand-new conclusion: "If all I'm doing is creating beautiful spaces, I'm failing. But if I'm creating beautiful spaces where families are thriving, then I'm really doing something." Doing that became my new calling.

The house really started to become a space where creativity flowed, and that set me down a new path in all of my design work. It's not just about pretty anymore. It's about practical. It's about children feeling that they can be at home. From then on, everything I'd touch from a design standpoint would have that element of balance to it—where it wasn't just aesthetically pleasing, but it also fit into my (or my client's) stage of life.

In seemingly no time at all, we had vegetables growing and a couple of chickens laying eggs. The boys loved their room with a windmill in it, and the girls loved their fifty-dollar "princess-style" chandelier from Lowe's that dangled from their ceiling.

The kids' living room featured a couple of big chalkboards and a beat-up old farm table where they could get creative to their little hearts' contents. I put some of those big old letters up on the walls of that room, spelling out "PLAY" on one wall and using everyone's first initial in an appropriate spot. Then I redid the kitchen with a clean black countertop and white subway tiles.

I filled that home with the beautiful sorts of things I loved, from an old wooden bench to bulky antique black candle sconces and some old gates on the walls and a cool-looking old antique scale that didn't serve any purpose other than to look old and cool.

I swear, the moment we moved into that house designed around *us*, I saw my family come alive in ways I'd never quite felt before. The kids were happy, and that made mama happy. Chip seemed all sorts of content to go out and feed his chickens in the morning. And I sometimes found it hard to believe that we'd had such a breakthrough as a family—and I'd had such a breakthrough as a designer and mom—in what was once an ugly, shotgun flip home.

It turned out that Chip's reasons for moving into that home were good ones. Change was good. It was inspirational. But that's not what I'm talking about. It's the other reasons he had—the notion that maybe the economy was slowing down a bit and maybe we ought to reduce our financial footprint—that proved to be a godsend. Because just as we started enjoying our new life in that Carriage Square home, our biggest investment ever took an unexpected turn that would rip the rug right out from under our feet.

# TWELVE

# GETTING TO THE BOTTOM

I picked up the phone and within two words I realized this was the type of call no businessman wants to receive.

It was my banker.

"Hi, Chip," he said. Even those first two words sounded shaky. "Hey, man, I've got some bad news," he continued. "But I don't want you to worry. We'll get through this."

Could there be a more chilling way to open a conversation? I couldn't imagine what we were about to "get through," and I was completely unprepared to hear the news he was about to tell me.

Months before this, Chip and I had basically gone and put all of our eggs into one big basket—and no, I'm not talking about the eggs we were collecting from Chip's chickens.

Over the past four years, we had gone from being these mom-and-pop remodelers and house flippers doing one, maybe two properties at a time to tackling five, eight, ten properties at a time. The Boys had grown into a big crew, and we had become masters of our trade. The economies of scale had finally tipped in our favor. The fact that we were buying building materials in bulk meant each individual project was a little more profitable than the last.

Right from the start, I'd been rolling the profits from one flip into the next. We wouldn't even see the money before it was gone, invested in the next one and the next. And every single time I did that, I made money. Anyone I borrowed from, whether it was my dad, a good friend, or an investor, made their money back plus interest every time. It seemed as though we had the Midas touch.

I'd learned so much by that point that I'd decided it was time to do what the big boys do. When my dad and I had sold the eleven acres to that big development firm, the guy I shook hands with wore a $50,000 Rolex. I didn't covet that watch, but I did envy his success. Now I was sure I, too, could handle that kind of big endeavor.

Doing a few houses at a time spread out all over town meant that a lot of money was being spent on separate crews and trucks and hauling things all over the place. The way to make money was to put a large development together with multiple homes all at once, all in one place.

So that's what I set my sights on. We basically stopped buying new flip homes and instead poured all of our money into developing this piece of land we'd been sitting on. The plan was to create a neighborhood called Magnolia Villas—thirty-eight comfortable, affordable little first-rate homes all designed by Jo. We'd even gone and opened up a real-estate arm of our company so that all the sales and sales commissions on this whole deal would come our way.

It was a good plan. It really was. But it takes a lot of money to put a plan like that together, and that meant putting all of our eggs into the proverbial basket and taking out a massive line of credit from the bank.

I'm not going to talk about the exact numbers here, but it was a huge line of credit that we'd budgeted every dollar for permits, roads, water and sewer lines, electric hookups, estimated building materials, and contracts with additional crews—all so we could get those houses built quickly and sell them in time to start paying back that line of credit from the profits. We had to do it quickly because, basically, every day that line of credit remained open, it represented a large amount of interest.

I trusted Chip completely with this. His instincts had been right every time we'd jumped into something new. Plus, I was excited about the homes themselves. With this newfound sense of purpose in my mission when it came to design, I drew up plans for the most adorable, functional, livable spaces I'd ever imagined. These were smaller homes, but I had plenty of firsthand experience with that. I knew how to design a small home that I could love, one that would be filled with open spaces and hideaway spaces and the kinds of textures and surfaces and little touches that would make a person feel welcome before he or she even opened the attractive solid-wood front door.

The problem is, there weren't going to be any doors or anything else. We got the plans all approved. We had the road crews come in to lay out and pave the streets. We had the sidewalks and gutters in place and all the proper drainage we needed in order to start building the actual houses.

And that's when our banker called with the bad news.

The tidal wave of economic despair that had swept through the rest of the country, that had already crippled housing developers in far-off places like Miami and Las Vegas, had finally reached Waco, Texas. The federal government had come in and told the banks they had no choice but to pull back on any pending loans and lines of credits. And not just pull back a little, but pull back by half.

"We don't have a choice about this," my banker told me.

The line of credit we needed to get the project completed had been suddenly cut in half. And if we couldn't complete the project, we would have no way to repay that loan.

And here's the thing: We had already received nearly half of that line of credit. We'd already used it to make nonrefundable down payments on everything we needed to get started. We had materials on site. There was no way out.

I'm sitting there going, "Jo, we're into this thing for a ton of money, and I've got most of the invoices sitting on my desk that are due to be paid—some in thirty days, some in forty-five days. What are we gonna do?"

Everyone we'd worked with up until that moment had been paid on time. So they had no idea we were standing on the edge of this cliff. No one had any idea that there was anything wrong. If we called them now, they'd all be hit just as hard and shockingly as we'd been hit by the bank's news.

My banker insisted he would help us get through it, and he did. We came up with a plan. We had managed to save some money that we had tied up in a CD, so we cashed that in. Our banker friend even waived the penalty so we wouldn't lose the little bit of interest we'd earned. Jo had some cash she'd been saving up on the side, too, just as she had way back when the shop was open. The banker was able to open us up a couple of smaller lines of credit so we could pay some bills while we tried to pull the rest together.

All of this took a lot of finagling and creative thinking. Those big developers in Miami or Las Vegas would have just wiped their hands of it, walked away, declared bankruptcy, and said "adios." In fact, many of them did. But Jo and I couldn't do that. We wouldn't do that. There was no way we were going to let anybody we'd made promises to not get paid.

After all of the scrambling, after everything was said and done, after we literally poured everything we had into trying to fix this thing, we were still $100,000 short of the finish line.

Chip and I prayed together. A lot. We were doing well in our new house. The kids were happy, and we did our best to hide our problems from them, even as our stomachs clenched at the breakfast table and we felt like breaking every time the mailman brought another stack of bills that we had absolutely no money left to pay.

It wasn't just a matter of paying construction bills now. We were literally tapped out. In a few weeks' time we would have nothing left to pay the electric bill and the mortgage on our home, where we lived with our children.

We were still working on some remodeling projects. In fact, I was doing the best work of my life, and we brought in some money through that work. But it wasn't nearly enough. So at that point, all of our praying led us to do something that felt completely radical to us.

I reached out to two friends of mine—and I'm using that term very loosely. These were people I didn't know well, people I'd worked with here and there. And they were fairly comfortable financially. Not rich—not by any means. But they were the type of people who might have some money in the bank and might be interested in earning a better return than the 1 percent the bank was giving them at the time.

I took these two guys to lunch, and as sick as I was on the inside and as much of a panic as I was in, I tried to keep the conversation all business. "So look: I'm in a bit of a pickle. It's not bad news, like I'm in this huge bind, but we do have this development called Magnolia Villas under way, and we would be interested in your financing the completion of it. The bank has essentially capped us at an amount that was much lower than what we had initially agreed on."

I explained what the status of the development was and what we had already done to raise the money. "I've got all the work on the ground, but I still need about $100,000 to get us across the finish line."

I asked them for $50,000 each and laid out some terms on how quickly we believed we'd be able to pay them back with interest. It was a very fair deal, and even though I'd kept it focused on the business aspects, I basically felt like I'd spilled my guts to those guys.

One of them was completely silent, just didn't say a word. The other guy said, "I don't know, man. It sounds too risky for me." He asked a lot of questions and seemed nervous about the deal in general.

I'd never had anybody react that way to a deal of mine, ever. It felt like a kick in the gut. In their defense, however, this is not what those guys did for a living. They were not angel investors or financial gurus. They were just good guys I thought might want to get in on this with us.

Long story short, they both walked away without much commitment and seemed generally uninterested. They were much better friends with each other than they were with me, and I just hoped that maybe the one who hadn't said a word was on my side and would convince his friend not to be so skeptical.

I walked away feeling like Russell Crowe's character in that boxer movie *Cinderella Man*. I wondered if I was going to have to be that formerly proud man who had once been at the top of my profession and now had to wander around to all of my old cronies with my hat in my hand, begging for a dollar so I could buy my kids some milk.

We decided we'd better sit down and go over everything again. We went through the old invoices that were still unpaid and the new ones that had come in since we got the news, and we realized that we now had $100,000 in invoices sitting there. So even if those two men decided to make the investment (which at this point seemed very unlikely), all of that money was already spent, and we'd be back to falling behind again the very next month unless we could presell some of the houses or encounter some other windfall.

A couple of very long days went by, and I finally got a call from the silent guy I'd taken to lunch. He said, "Hey, man, I really want to see the development. My wife and I want to meet you out there and walk the property and just get a better sense of what exactly you're talking about."

So we met them over at the site, and these two walked around just as calm as they could be. "This is beautiful," they said. "This is awesome," they said.

"Wow," I said. "I was hoping you would think that. So what are you guys doing? Why did you want to come walk the site?"

"I know that meeting was a bit rough the other day," he said. "I just want you to know that I've never done this kind of thing before. But when you were talking, you were really speaking my language. I admire how hard you've fought to keep the project alive and make sure everyone gets paid, and I was actually eager to help you out. But I wasn't sure if it was just my heart talking, you know? So I went back and told my wife about it, and we prayed about this. And, well, we've decided that we want to give you the $100,000."

I reminded him that I only felt comfortable with the $50K investment to spread out the risk.

"I know, but we prayed about it, and we just feel this is the right thing to do. You're doing a good thing here. We need this kind of development in Waco, and we have no doubt you're going to sell all of these houses and it will make a big difference to a lot of people.

"And if you don't? Well, as I said, we've prayed a lot about this, so we don't want you to worry if you don't ever pay us back. We've already imagined that, so if this doesn't work out like you hoped it would, don't worry about it. We're already over it. We don't want this to be awkward as far as our relationship is concerned."

My knees almost gave out. It took everything in me not to break down right then and there. This wasn't like a best friend who would bend over backward to bail you out of trouble. They were just acquaintances at the time. So for them to say something like that came as a complete shock. They had that $100,000 check with them, and they handed it to us right then and there.

The two of us went home in absolute awe of what had just happened. Then we sat down and considered how best to use that money. There were a number of invoices that were due in two days. But for a moment, we wondered if maybe we should invest the money in a quick flip house, something that might turn that money into $150,000 and give us some leeway to pay other bills. But that would mean putting some people off by thirty days or more, and that just didn't feel right to us.

So what did we do?

We both looked at each other and said, "Give it away."

We didn't mean "give it away" in the sense of philanthropy, but in recognizing that this money wasn't ours. It was owed to others. So we sat down and wrote out $100,000 worth of checks. We were completely broke again within a week, but everybody got paid. Every bill was up to date. With that check, we were able to buy ourselves another month or so of time to get back on our feet. It's sad looking back, because even with a miracle like that, we still had our doubts.

We both realized quickly thereafter that this was no fluke. It had been the story of our life together, ever since we'd met. From the very beginning, I feel like we had encountered miracle after miracle that allowed us to get by and survive. Now it was happening on a much bigger scale—in hundred-thousand-dollar increments. But maybe we should have been paying more attention to those little miracles all along. We were now *both* out on that limb, and we looked up and saw God right there with us.

Somehow we were always wily enough to get ourselves out of a financial pickle by finding the money from somewhere. Or so I'd thought. But this was not us being "wily." This couldn't be anything but the grace of God.

Did those earlier "breaks" come from the same source?

Getting that $100,000 check just made us open our eyes and see that whenever we'd needed a break, when a house would sell or rent would come through just in the nick of time—God was there orchestrating. We were just so overwhelmed with all this.

Maybe getting to the bottom all those times, and especially that time, was some sort of a test. A test of will maybe, a test of faith, a test of our resolve to stay the course in following our dreams and to do the right thing when it came to how we treated others. I don't know.

What I do know, looking back on it now, is that all of these big, life-changing things were right around the corner for us at that moment. And if we'd given up, if we'd walked away, if we'd crumbled when we were at our lowest, we never would have made it around the corner to see all of the blessings that were about to come due.

# THIRTEEN

# SURVIVING OR THRIVING

I'm not sure what it was about moving into that little shotgun of a house that brought so many revelations to the surface. But right in the middle of our financial crisis, I had yet another awakening—a true lightbulb moment, just as I'd had when I decided to design our living space for *us*. And this new revelation was also sparked by the laughter of my children down the hall.

I'd managed to put that house together in a way that made my family happier than perhaps we'd ever been. We all had space to be ourselves and to be together, even though this home was half the size of our previous one. The only problem I seemed to keep running into in that smaller space was that there just wasn't enough room to keep all our stuff contained. Even though the kids had their own living room, everything still seemed to spill out everywhere all the time.

I was still working hard to make this house perfect, which to me meant not only giving it some character and bringing it to life, but also keeping it clean and uncluttered. And it seemed as if all day, every day, I spent most of my time picking up after the kids, yelling at them whenever they spilled a glass of milk, then mopping the floors one more time. It was exhausting.

I was finally taking a moment for myself one afternoon, plopping down on our old sofa with the new slipcover, when I made the mistake of looking down. My beautiful, brand-new, snowy-white slipcover was covered in little black fingerprints. I mean, there were fingerprints everywhere.

I looked up and noticed that the whole house was messy again—a shoe here, a sock there, a pile of toys on the coffee table. I had already spent half the day cleaning. And everything in me wanted to stand up and go yell at those kids for not washing their hands like I'd told them to a thousand times. I also started yelling at myself in my mind: *What mother in her right mind would buy white slipcovers for a sofa with four little kids in the house? I mean, really. White?* I was so mad at myself and the kids that I was just about to lose it.

Then I heard the kids down the hall.

They were playing in one of the bedrooms, and the whole lot of them erupted in laughter over some silly thing. Their giggles were so full of joy. The sound of their little voices pierced my heart.

I looked back down at all of those tiny fingerprints on my white slipcover, and I realized something surprising: *Someday I might actually miss those little fingerprints.*

Right then and there, I knew I had been focused on the wrong things. And I realized I had a choice to make.

I could go in there and yell, ruining their little moment and then having to spend another hour of my life trying to clean up the mess that they'd made. Or I could choose to let it go. I could go play with my kids and maybe get a chance to share in that laughter right alongside them.

So what if my house wasn't perfect?

It was perfect just the way it was.

I realized that my determination to make things perfect meant I was chasing an empty obsession all day long. Nothing was ever going to be perfect the way I had envisioned it in the past. Did I want to keep spending my energy on that effort, or did I want to step out of that obsession and to enjoy my kids, maybe allowing myself to get messy right along with them in the process?

I chose the latter—and that made all the difference.

This revelation was so much more than a lightbulb turning on in my head. I felt as if a hundred pounds got lifted off my shoulders that afternoon. I remember sitting there on that sofa going, "Holy cow. I can breathe."

It all came down to a mind shift in which I asked myself, "What am I *going for* in life?" Was it to achieve somebody else's idea of what a perfect home should look like? Or was it to live fully in the perfection of the home and family I have?

My revelation wouldn't mean that I would never clean my house again. It wouldn't even keep me from throwing that slipcover in the washing machine—eventually. My kids do tend to play better and act better in a clean environment, and Chip appreciates a clean home too. My family inspires me to want to keep our home clean for them, and I personally can't think straight in an environment that's too cluttered. And yet the time I spend with my kids is worth far more than the time I spend cleaning.

Right then and there, I made up my mind to stop cleaning the house during the day. If that meant I had to stay up an extra forty-five minutes at night doing dishes or cleaning up the living room after the kids were in bed, then so be it. I also vowed to set up better storage systems and to teach the kids that everything had a place. But I wasn't going to obsess about any of that. Not anymore.

That day changed me. It really did. And I quickly found that my shift in mind-set had a positive effect on our life together. Now when someone spills a glass of milk, I don't worry so much about the mess. Instead, I try to focus on my relationship with the one who spilled the milk.

I still have my bad days, believe me, when I see that milk for the mess that it is and I yell, "Oh, come on!" I get mad. I'm not perfect. But I recognize now that yelling is always the lesser of two options. The better option is to use that moment to teach them, "Well, you know what? I did that when I was a kid too. We all make mistakes." Followed by, "How about you help me clean this up?"

What I've found is that something as common as spilled milk can turn into a rich moment with my kids. And for years my misguided perfectionism robbed both them and me of those moments. And I can't help but wonder how many other moments I robbed from my kids and from my husband while trying to attain some vision of a perfect home that I was never going to attain anyway.

Before my slipcover revelation, I never allowed the kids to paint or do projects on my dining-room table because it was my "favorite table." Today, not only do I let them do their projects there, but I'm the one who instigates it. "Okay, we're going to paint, kids!" Why? Because I replaced that "perfect" table with one that's all scuffed up and only gets better looking with age.

I also tried to set aside various spots throughout that home where my kids were *expected* to make a mess: in their living room, on that table I just mentioned, I even carved out a spot in the kitchen where they could cook and have fun experimenting with food. That way I could be prepared, which means I wouldn't overreact. And that in turn meant my kids could be kids, and I could be a better mom. It was all connected.

The funny thing to me is that whenever we had people step foot into our house after that, they seemed more wowed by it than any other house I'd designed or lived in—including the 1920s dream house in Castle Heights.

That got me thinking about the pressure we women and moms are all under these days. It seems as if the standards are so much higher than they were just a few years ago, mainly because of what we see whenever we look on the Internet.

It used to require some effort to feel like an inferior mom and wife. A woman would have to go to a newsstand and spend six dollars on a magazine to see the current societal standard of "What my family and home are supposed to look like." Now it just shows up on social media everywhere you look, and it always seems to be picture-perfect. That's all anyone seems to post—perfect pictures of perfect families enjoying perfect moments.

Along with that, I think everyone's expectations of themselves have gotten so much higher. I mean, honestly, as a stay-at-home mom, every time I had a moment to open Facebook or Pinterest I would walk away thinking, *I'm not doing enough.* And then I'd start second-guessing myself. I think that's what I started to overcome with those revelations in my own home.

It's funny that these revelatory moments of mine happened on couches in two different houses, and I wonder why that is. But I don't have to wonder about the *results* of those moments.

Shortly after I sat on the couch at the Castle Heights house and really noticed for the first time that I wasn't happy, even though I'd worked so hard to make everything look perfect, I had a conversation with a friend of mine. I was exhausted all of the time, and I said to this friend: "I feel like I'm just surviving at this point. I'm not thriving."

Once I was in the Carriage Square house and embracing the laughter and messiness of my kids and not cleaning all day long, I realized that it was up to me to flip that switch from surviving to thriving. It was just a mental shift, a readjustment in my way of thinking—like seeing my kids' fingerprints as kind of cute instead of a miserable mess.

I actually made that particular mental shift right after I had my Carriage Square revelation. It happened instantly—just like that—right after I made the decision to enjoy my kids instead of obsessing over making everything perfect. I looked down at those fingerprints—I was still on the couch—and suddenly they looked completely different.

Then I got to thinking about the bigger picture: If I'm going to sit around and say I am "just surviving" every day, well, guess what? When a big wave comes along suddenly, I won't be surviving—I'll be drowning!

I mean, that's life. Life is never predictable. Life is never really manageable. If your mind-set is always, "I'm just surviving," it seems to me that would wind up being your mind-set for the rest of your life. You'd just get stuck in it.

So I finally flipped the switch in my mind. I said, "I have to choose to thrive, even in the pain. Even when it's tough." And it *was* tough. While I was coming to this conclusion, we were right in the middle of our whole financial mess. We'd managed to escape just under the wire through that God-given $100,000 check, but we were still in trouble.

The miracle of that breakthrough moment for me is that I didn't really let our situation get to me. I didn't wallow in it. I didn't allow it to dictate my happiness. I was scared, sure. But for now at least, we had our house; we had our kids; we had our health; and we were living this beautiful life together. And I told myself, "I want to make all that count in this season, because otherwise it's just going to be a waste."

I didn't want to look back at this experience and regret how I handled it. I wanted to say, win or lose, that we believed in love, that we had faith, and in essence we fought the good fight. I didn't want to be found a quitter or a doubter. None of these things would have been helpful to Chip anyway. So even though I didn't feel it some days, and even though I shed my fair share of tears, I woke up every day and told myself, "We can do this. God has not brought us this far to let us down now." And I would tell Chip, "You got this. Most guys would collapse under this pressure, but you were built for this!"

This paradigm shift seemed to work, and I know Chip appreciated it. As a parent, as a wife, as a business owner, I simply decided: "I'm not going to survive anymore. I'm going to thrive."

It wasn't some big life-altering change that was difficult to achieve, either. It was instantaneous. I just realized that I had a choice to make in every moment, on every day, with every decision.

I made that choice, when the next glass of milk was spilled, to choose a thriving response rather than the surviving one. And I made that choice when another gigantic bill landed in our mailbox that day after the last of our $100,000 miracle was spent. Was I going to just survive this? Or was I going to get with my husband and think this through so we could overcome it together and thrive?

I still had my moments when I'd make the wrong choice and get all fed up and start fussing at the kids or Chip or start beating myself up over some mistake I'd made. But the more I kept asking myself that question—the more I focused on thriving—the shorter those "just surviving" moments seemed to last.

There was something in that low point with our business that drew Jo and me closer together. My usual optimism seemed to slip. I wasn't sure we were going to find our way out of this one. But she took on this really positive attitude about everything that helped me get through it.

I always said, "When things come against us we can either turn on each other, or we can come together and turn on it."

We almost started to reverse roles in that season, where she was the one telling me that it was all going to be all right and that even if it wasn't, then that would be all right too. We were together, and our kids were good, and that was all that mattered. We were thriving—that was the way she put it.

I wasn't sure I believed her, to be honest. I was terrified we were about to lose everything. But the irony of it all is that just as we hit a low point where I thought we might slip into bankruptcy any day, the local newspaper caught wind of what we were doing with our development and decided to do a front-page story about us: "What a neat thing you're doing over on that side of town. You guys want to be in the paper?"

I didn't focus on our problems when I talked to that reporter. I just described all of the pros of this development and what a great project it was for that area of town and for Waco in general. I hoped the buzz would convince someone that one of the Magnolia Villas houses would be perfect for them. That would mean we could actually start building them and maybe start selling some.

The article came out, and a couple of days later, a lawyer in town called me up. He told me his mother was living out on some acreage outside of town, and she needed a home that was smaller and closer to everything and easier to manage. We talked for a few minutes about what we were planning, and I told him why I thought one of the villas might be perfect for her, and by the end of the conversation he said, "I want one."

"You want one?"

"Yeah. How much is it?"

"Well, the model that sounds right for your mom is $176,000 and change."

"Great. Okay, meet me at my office on Wednesday and bring the contract."

"Okay, great," I echoed.

Now, the way things usually work, somebody wants to read the contract and get a second opinion and then bargain with you on the price. Then, even after they sign an agreement to buy the place, there are usually contingencies, and they have to take whatever down payment they have and go out and secure a loan. It's a long, slow process that sometimes ends with nothing happening. So I didn't get my hopes up too much about that one. But I was encouraged, and I was even more encouraged when the front-page article resulted in dozens of calls just like that one. I felt like we were on our way.

I went ahead and met with this new lead and I handed him the contract. He started reading it over. "Let's see. Yep. All right. This is just a simple residential contract. So, you ready?"

I said, "Yeah. I'm ready to rock. So you're telling me you're gonna be our first Villa? Wow, this is such a big deal. Thank you, man. I appreciate it!"

"No sweat. I'm going to sign right here, and if you don't mind signing right now, I'll have my secretary make some copies."

I signed, and he signed, and he handed it to his secretary. I stepped out to use the restroom. And when I came back, I found that this man had written out a check for the full amount and stuck it under a little paper clip with the contract.

"All right," he said. "Go build Mom a great house. When do you think this will be ready? You think four to six months ought to do it?"

"Yes, sir. I promise. It will be four months if we're lucky—six months worst-case scenario if we hit some bad weather or something. But I'll let you know. Thank you. Your mom's gonna be thrilled. I promise."

I was walking on air when I left that office. It wasn't just because the attorney's check would allow us to catch up and begin to move forward with the rest of the development. I also knew that selling one of those villas sight-unseen would be all the kick-start we needed to eventually sell the rest of them.

People don't like to shop at a strip mall with one store in it or to eat at a restaurant with only one car in the parking lot. They like to see action, activity, excitement—and that's what we were going to have at Magnolia Villas. This one build meant we'd have a crew out there now, visibly working and building a beautiful house for everyone to see as they passed by on Bosque Boulevard.

Oh, we forgot to mention that. This development we were trying to build just happened to be right off Bosque Boulevard—the very same Bosque Boulevard where my shop once stood and where our headquarters for Magnolia Homes was still standing. It felt like something more than coincidence to us that we finally had a heartbeat for Magnolia Villas on that very same artery, just a little further to the west.

Anyway, we were so excited about making this the perfect house for that attorney's mother that we wound up calling her and offering to meet with her so I could show her some paint colors and finishes and design the interior exactly to her liking.

The woman's name was Peggy, and as her son, Dale Williams, had told Chip, she lived on a forty-acre farm about ten minutes outside of town.

The first time we drove up there, we didn't think much of it. It was all about the business of finding out what this sweet woman wanted in her home. She invited us to come back up again and have coffee with her and said we should bring the kids. So we did. This property was pretty. There were some beautiful oak trees, and forty acres is forty acres—it's nice to see all of that open land after living in the crowded way most of us live. But this wasn't a farm with white fences or a beautiful farmhouse up on a bluff somewhere. It was all chain-link and barbed wire. The house was old and needed a lot of work. It just wasn't anything that grabbed Chip or me around the collars and said, "Hey! Buy this!"

We knew that Peggy would be selling the place once she moved into her new villa, so you would think the two of us would have been looking at that property as something we could flip, at the very least. But we weren't. I mean, I tend to be a love-at-first-sight kinda guy when it comes to houses, and I just wasn't in love with it.

When the kids were all standing there at the end of the second visit, Peggy asked if they'd like to come back and play on her farm again. And the kids all said, "Yes, ma'am!" We'd been inside talking to Peggy and hadn't even noticed how much fun they were having in that yard, so we were taken aback by their enthusiasm. "Well," Peggy said, "next time y'all should go down and have a picnic in the pecan orchard."

"Pecan orchard?" Chip asked.

"There's a cluster of about twenty hundred-year-old pecan trees out back. It's a real nice spot for a picnic. Go down there next time," Peggy said.

So we did. We came back and had a lovely picnic under the pecan trees, and Chip and I both started to see this land in a whole other light. That night the two of us started dreaming together, just as we'd done back in the early days of our marriage.

"Can you imagine what it would be like to live on a farm?"

"Imagine how many chickens I could have on a place like this?" Chip said. He sounded like a little kid. "We could get goats. Cows, even!"

"*You* could get goats and cows, sure. As long as I don't have to take care of them."

"Oh, babe, you wouldn't have to lift a finger. I *want* to take care of 'em!" he said.

I of course started seeing the possibilities for that old turn-of-the-century farmhouse. I imagined what was under those walls and what those wide-plank floors might look like if they were refinished. I imagined an addition. I imagined opening it up, moving the walls around, doing my best to give the kids plenty of space to run and slide in there, the way they did in the hallway at our current house.

Then we really got to dreaming: With all of that land, maybe we could put up a cool tree house. I could do more than just garden; I could build a greenhouse so I could garden year-round. We could get dogs again and let them run around free without the worry of neighbors trying to get us thrown in jail.

"I wonder how much they'll want for the place," Chip asked out loud. The fact that he'd said it out loud made it seem like a real possibility. Like he was thinking the same thing I was—how perfect this place would be to raise our family.

Peggy was kind enough to invite us to use that land anytime we wanted. "You don't even need to stop in and say hi. Just treat it like your own," she said. So we did. We went up to that property about once a week with the kids, letting them run around and stretch their legs and get fresh air. And as construction on Peggy's villa was nearly complete, Chip found himself completely inundated with Magnolia Villa contracts and prospects.

The whole idea that even a small rock can start an avalanche was certainly playing out here. Villas were popping up like crazy. The lots were selling, and contracts were coming in steadily now after all that exposure in the local paper. Things were really rolling. So months after we'd started going to Peggy's farm fairly frequently, Chip finally got the nerve to ask her son what the asking price for the property might be.

He said without hesitation that he hoped it would go for around half a million dollars—half a million that we didn't have and couldn't even hope to borrow. Because of what had happened with the Villas, our credit was all tapped out. We would be lucky to get a loan on half that much. We couldn't even get new loans for flips or renovations. The glory days of using bank money to finance our dreams seemed to be over. Even with things flying over at the Villas, the banks needed more proof that they weren't going to end up stalling out.

Still, we fell so in love with that land—not to mention the idea of what I could turn that house into—that we didn't want to let go. Chip kept talking to the attorney, who really acted a bit like a confidant or an advisor in that season. We decided to put our Carriage Square house on the market, just in case there was an off chance we could make this work. We figured that with all of the renovations I'd done we would be able to turn a nice profit, and maybe that would give us enough of a down payment to get a loan. If we could get the attorney and his mother to lower the asking price on the farm, we just might be able to make the deal work.

We worked out all the numbers and came to a pretty depressing conclusion. Even if we got our full asking price for the Carriage Square house, we'd still be well under the asking price they hoped for.

The thing is, we'd actually grown pretty close to our attorney friend and his beautiful mother through all of those visits and talks. We learned that he was about our parents' age and he loved that farm and had all sorts of fond memories of his dad there. The farm was called Covey Rise Ranch—named after a covey of quail. His dad had raised quail dogs on that property—gorgeous bird dogs that he and his dad had spent hours working in those fields.

Chip finally got the nerve to make them an offer, which they promptly turned down. But they did say they weren't in a hurry and if anything changed for us financially we should definitely reapproach them.

Peggy left the farm and moved into her villa, and she loved it. It was the perfect size, the perfect layout, and she loved the location. She just could not rave enough about that house. We were happy for her. But even as more offers came in for the sale of the villas, we weren't close enough to paying off our debt or making enough money to allow us to make a better offer on her property for ourselves.

We continued to visit the property pretty often. The kids loved it. We loved it. We just wanted to hold on to our enjoyment of it as long as we could. And one week we were actually sitting on a bench on the front porch of that old farmhouse, with the kids running around the yard, when Chip got a call on his cell phone.

"Yeah. Yes. Tell them we accept," I heard him say.

When he hung up the phone, he told me, "We just got an offer on the house. It's a good offer. A really good offer. I said we'd take it."

And here's where things just get crazy. Jo and I believe in miracles, but when we hear stories like this we usually go, "Yeah right. Like that happened!" But as sure as I'm sitting here writing this, my phone rang less than ten minutes later. It was Peggy's son.

This intelligent, tough lawyer said, "Chip, you know what? I've been thinking about that offer, and I don't know. My mom is happy over in the Villas. You guys did her right with that house." He spoke as if we'd done her this great big favor by building her a nice home, when in fact they'd been the ones who'd trusted us that the Villas were going to be great.

"So, if you really want the farm, you've got yourself a deal. I'll give it to you for the amount you mentioned before. I can see you and your family loving it out there." Little did he know that "out there" was where we were sitting at that very moment!

"Oh, wow! That's fantastic," Chip said, standing right up with the biggest smile on his face. I got tears in my eyes just seeing Chip's expression. I stood up, and he gave me a great big hug with that phone still to his ear.

"Uh-huh," he said. "Uh-huh. Wow. You're kidding! I don't even know what to say. Thank you. Thank you so much."

I got off the phone and said, "Jo, you're not going to believe this. Not only is he going to sell us this place, but he's wanting to owner-finance it. He said he would actually prefer a little interest on the money, and he felt like this was the best deal for now, and we could finance him out in a couple years when the Villas were closer to being completed.'

Jo said, "What?" At this point we were literally in shock. The kids even noticed that something was going on and came running over to see what was happening.

"Kids," I said, as Drake, Ella, Duke, and little Emmie all gathered around us. "How would you like it if the farm was our home?"

"Yeah!" they all screamed. They started running around hooting and hollering.

I simply couldn't believe it. It was far beyond anything I'd ever imagined could actually happen in my life.

"Chip," I said. "We're buying a farm."

# FOURTEEN

# HEEDING THE CALL

Before we signed papers on the sale of our Carriage Square home, and just before we passed papers to buy Peggy's farm, my phone rang. On the other end of the line was the woman from a television production company who had the crazy idea to put Chip and me on TV.

It was two weeks later that the camera crew arrived, a few days after that when the houseboat arrived that Chip "surprised" me with and the top guy on the crew told us, "If I do my job, you two just landed yourself a reality TV show."

It was 2012 by the time an even bigger camera crew came back to film a full pilot episode of *Fixer Upper* for HGTV, and it wouldn't be until 2013 that the show would get picked up.

But we never stopped. We never slowed down. Our family just kept pushing, finding our way through. We didn't know if the TV show would ever really get off the ground. So we just kept working at making the most of our lives, despite a seemingly never-ending spate of financial obstacles.

Since the houseboat wasn't a livable option, my parents let us move into their house. They had actually bought a place in Castle Heights but later decided to move. Though they'd recently put the house on the market, it hadn't yet sold. So they said, "Hey, we know you're working on the farm. Why don't you just live in our house for a while? We don't have to sell it tomorrow."

The timing worked out great, and we were so thankful. It worked out well for the pilot episode, too, since we were right in the middle of renovating the farm, and that made for some good TV. It showed how we were starting over, starting fresh, turning something that was outdated into the home of our dreams, just like we do for our clients.

We loved being outside so much at the farm that the first thing Jo had me build was the big outdoor fireplace. We built the whole thing out of antique bricks we had found. She also got started on a garden. The house became the secondary concern. Every time we got some cash together and went out there to do some remodeling, we always ended up doing another project outside. I guess subconsciously we decided we'd just take it slow and do what we could when we could, which was definitely a change of pace from our normal routine.

We would drive out to the country and sit at what felt like our vacation home, only this vacation home needed a boatload of work. We would sit beside the fire and Jo would tend her garden. And then we would go inside and just mess around, trying to figure out what we could do with whatever money we had coming in.

We knew we needed to expand the house some. We were eventually able to figure out how to create a lot of room upstairs in the attic, which was unused space at the time. But before we built anything out, we ripped things apart hoping to find some old beams and hardwood floors. And when we tore off the drywall, we found shiplap everywhere. So I was instantly like, "We're using that as our finished wall." We painted it all white and didn't bother filling in any of the nail holes or anything. The way I saw it, every one of those nail holes was a little piece of history, and they all added character to the home. And just as important, we saved eight grand in drywall costs right there.

We were always thrifty, and we loved using old materials, making our own things, doing the work ourselves when we could. It was our job.

**It was our passion. And this farm was our dream. We couldn't wait until it was time to move in.**

Back in the late 1800s, when a place like this was originally built, you had to work with what you had, and you had to figure stuff out. You certainly couldn't Google it. You didn't have Internet. You didn't even have how-to books. You had to sit there and wrestle with it. You found this old spare part, you did this other thing, you hooked it up to a donkey, and you tried it out.

Sometimes it worked. Sometimes it didn't. But eventually you'd pop out on the other side and say, "I've got this."

Call me old-fashioned, but I've always solved problems like that.

**It took us quite a while before we made things happen at the farm and got it to a point that it was move-in ready. Then we stopped and looked back at all we'd done, the good times and the bad. The times when we were literally flush with cash and the times we could barely pay our bills.**

**Did this mean we were finally out of the woods? It sure felt like it. We had managed to keep our heads above water through some really tough times. And even in those tough times our precious employees had continued to play a huge part in our business. They stuck it out with us.**

Some of these employees went way back with us, all the way to the beginning. Most of the Boys who'd helped with my early flips were still around. You probably know a couple of them—Shorty and José— from the show. Even before that, one of the guys who mowed lawns with me, ironically, was Shorty and José's father-in-law. His daughter was the first girl I ever hired to help run the little corner wash-and-fold business. She's still with us today—we don't own the wash-and-fold anymore, but she works for our company. So does Jo's friend who worked with her before she decided to close the shop.

Looking back, it's amazing to see how it all ties together. Those people had seen how hard we'd worked to always pay them first, no matter what, during all the tough times. Without even purposefully trying, just by being who we are and doing what we do, we'd created a Magnolia family.

The work we did managed to touch a lot of people's lives, and it's just not possible to put into words the gratitude we feel for each and every person who's helped us along the way.

A couple of our suppliers bent over backward for us during those lean times too. A few of them gave us extra time to pay for some of the materials we needed in order to keep going.

They say it takes a village to raise a child. I'd like to amend that and say it takes a village to run a small business!

We are glad we doubled down on our renovation business during that tough period. We focused heavily on the real-estate side of our Magnolia Homes business, too, both listing and selling homes in and around Waco and helping buyers find the home of their dreams. We especially liked it when we could find our customers a home that wasn't quite move-in ready but was in their price range. Then we could offer our renovation services as a way to turn that fixer-upper into a home they would love. Not only were jobs like that fun and fulfilling; they also allowed us to put all of our skills to work—and they were the jobs that kept us afloat financially.

Well, guess what? That evolving business model was just the thing that pushed the concept of a Chip-and-Joanna TV show over the top. The folks at HGTV loved the idea of following home buyers through the process from start to finish, from selection through renovation, with a big reveal at the end when they finally saw the finished product.

I find it interesting that the skills we honed flipping houses had prepared us for the grueling time commitments involved with film-ing client-based renovations for television. They said all this made for "great TV." I mean, the timing of it all couldn't have worked out any better. As with the sizzle reel, we couldn't have scripted any of these things if we tried.

We didn't know what made "great TV." We were just trying to make a living and trying hard to honor the craft we had both fallen in love with over the years.

We'd been in business for more than ten years, and by then I think people in Waco had come to know who we were and what we were all about. So when some of this started hitting, Waco seemed to support us and protect us. We were not stars here. We were just the same Chip and JoJo they'd known and supported for years.

I also love the fact that we had never quit.

We fought like cats and dogs to the bitter end, and one thing led to the other. Next thing you know, the remodeling business was booming, our flips were flipping, rentals were renting, and banks started lending again. All that happened right around the time the TV show got picked up in 2013.

Then all of a sudden we had these camera crews around us, and all these assistant directors and sound guys and production assistants and network executives were telling us how unique we were, and how they loved our work, and how great this TV show was going to be. It was all just surreal, like one of those dreams where you can't tell fact from fiction.

Honestly, I needed that boost after going through all of those ups and downs. I just felt vindicated. We'd spent all this time doing the best we could every day, and for people to notice it was just very rewarding.

It was certainly not about the money. There are very talented artists and craftsmen of all sorts who do amazing work and aren't rich. But for us to come out on the other side having a little money again and having some accolades coming in—yeah, it was nice.

One thing we were excited to do was to get Peggy's son his money, to refinance that owner-financed loan he'd been so generous to extend to us. He had been so patient, but now the Villas were in a great place. That made it much easier for the banks to take him out—finally. Which is exactly what he'd said would happen.

As things continued to improve and our business got healthier and healthier, we wanted to get one last thing cleared up. So, we called up the couple who had loaned us the $100,000 that allowed us to keep going during that terrible downturn. "Hey," we said when they answered the phone. "We were in the neighborhood. Do you mind if we come by and say hi?"

We had originally told them that our intention was to pay that money back within a year. When that year came and went and we told them it would take a while longer, they didn't fuss one bit. In fact, they reiterated their original position. Their generosity was crippling. In a world full of contracts and legalities, they could have chosen to throw the terms of this deal in our face, but instead they chose to be gracious and patient as we worked this out.

We stopped by that day and we handed them a check for $130,000.

I said, "Even though this is what we agreed on, I just want you to know I feel like I owe you infinitely more than that. You both have meant the world to us. We wouldn't even be here if it weren't for you."

They both got tears in their eyes. "This came at just the right time."

As I've mentioned, they weren't independently wealthy people, and it turns out they were in a spot where they needed to make some decisions for their family. Having that money at their disposal was going to help make those decisions easier.

Getting both of those loans taken care of felt so good. Those were people who had bent over backward for us. We honestly wouldn't even be here talking about any of this if it weren't for them.

Want to hear something even more interesting? When it came to the couple who loaned us that money, we wound up circling back with them. A year after we paid them back, they came to us looking to buy a new house. They even came with a big renovation budget to work with. And guess how much they budgeted for renovations? $130,000. They turned right around and sank that exact amount of money into their dream home. What are the chances? These circumstances were woven in such a way that you had to just sit back and marvel.

Most things in life are just beyond our planning and our control. Even when it comes to the farm, back when we first fell in love with the land, we had all sorts of doubts about spending more money than we had in order to buy it.

"We shouldn't be doing this," we said.

"Is this stupid?" we wondered.

But now both of us agree: God allowed Peggy's son to owner-finance that for us. He knew that in this season of life we were about to encounter, we would need a place to retreat to, where our kids could be away from it all and we could center ourselves. We truly believe that God put those plans in action because he knew what we would need as a family, even though we didn't have any clue what we needed ourselves.

How could we have possibly known that bringing some cameras in to film Chip and me at work and at home on the farm would turn into a big hit TV show? Apparently other people knew. The network people were confident about it. But we certainly didn't know.

From what we'd heard, reality TV shows were all about people yelling and screaming and flipping tables over for the cameras. What we would come to learn is that every show is different; every situation is unique. The network didn't ask us to do anything other than be ourselves.

What we learned from being around the folks at HGTV is that shows that have a heart behind them and are authentic tend to have the most loyal audiences. The other thing we have learned about television is we are thankful to be associated with HGTV and with High Noon Entertainment, the production company that films our show. Both have been good to us. They have honored our family, our story, and our town. They didn't have to do that. And no matter how this all shakes out, we will be forever grateful to them for allowing us to tell *our* story.

I have to say I'm glad authenticity is something they wanted, because that was all they were going to get from Chip and me. Nobody could ever script Chip Carter Gaines, even if they tried. And I would never have signed on if I couldn't be myself. I've come way too far in my life and career to compromise now, and for HGTV to allow us to be faithful to who we are and to showcase our business and our expertise has been an absolute honor.

We love our kids, we love each other, we love this town, and we love our clients. That's the heart behind our show. We're a real couple and a real company, and we do real jobs for people with real budgets. When there's heart and substance on a TV show, the drama just isn't needed.

What we do on camera is what we do in real life.

Well, there is one exception: that big canvas. We love to surprise our clients, but we'd never done that before, of course.

Chip and the producer came up with that idea at the very last minute when we were working on the pilot. There was a problem as to how to surprise the client, and as always, Chip got with the Boys and figured it out. I suppose that could be considered a bit of "drama" that we added to the show. But even that came from the heart.

It never gets old—that moment when we pull back that picture and we see our clients' faces as they experience their fixed-up new home for the very first time. We've spent weeks, sometimes months, getting to know these people, and it's just very moving to us to make them happy. Chip and I both know how important home is, and we love sharing that feeling with them.

That we get to have a show like this on national television, doing exactly what we're passionate about, is really a gift. They left it unscripted from the start, and I think people feel that. This is just our life!

I mean, honestly, I don't think there's anyone on television who'd pick up a dead cockroach off the floor and pop it into his mouth on camera. My husband is that guy. He has *always* been that guy—especially when fifty bucks is on the line. Come hang out with a bunch of his old college buddies sometime and listen to their "Chip stories," and you'll know for certain that the Chip you see on TV is the same Chip we all see at home. He just has a way of making things fun.

There are times at the end of a long day in front of the cameras when I just want to be done. It's a lot of work to not only do our job but also keep our energy up and try to get what they need for the cameras. But Chip will extend our day even further by annoying the heck out of me—trying out bad jokes and performing silly antics while the cameras are rolling, just to keep it amusing.

If it wasn't for him making me laugh, though, I might just work myself to death.

That's another funny thing that's changed since we moved to the farm: Jo seems to work twice as hard as I do now. She always has ten things going on. I used to be the one sort of juggling a million things at once, but now I've slowed down a little bit and she's sped up. It's interesting how roles can change like that.

I think that's just part of what's come along with the kids getting older too. Once they were in school, it became a whole lot easier to get work done outside the home. But being dedicated to our kids also meant we had to keep this TV show thing close to home. That meant setting some ground rules early on.

We carved out certain hours each day that we needed to set aside for family and business and insisted we would never travel more than thirty minutes outside of the Waco area for our renovation projects. We needed to be home for our kids, and their needs were going to come first as much as humanly possible.

We did try to be flexible, of course, knowing they were spending a lot of money to shoot this show and paying that whole professional crew who showed up in Waco with all of their equipment and trucks and union rules. So some compromise seemed in order. But we've still tried to stick to our ground rules as much as possible, even after the show took off and we knew it was a hit.

Honestly, we had no idea what we were in for.

No idea at all. The pilot alone earned big ratings when they aired it in May of 2013.

Everyone at the network got pretty excited.

But once the first episode of the series aired in April of 2014, the show just took off. I mean, took off like wildfire. Suddenly we were being recognized even when we left Waco. People were stopping us in stores and coming up to us at restaurants. I didn't know so many people watched HGTV. And I couldn't believe how many people had seen our show.

We still don't own a TV, so the only way we knew when a show was on—if we didn't go to a friend's house to watch—was when our phones would blow up with texts of congratulations or when e-mails would begin streaming in from all over the country asking us to do remodels.

We started getting all sorts of interview requests, and folks were asking us to speak at their events or their churches. It was absolutely crazy. Overnight our lives were turned upside down.

I was just real thankful we had the peace and quiet of the farm to go back to at the end of every day. It really did become our sanctuary.

Our home became more important than it had ever been. As we said a little earlier, I think God knew that place was exactly what our family needed in this new season. I am just so grateful for so many of the things we accomplished and even the challenges we went through before we landed on TV. Truly, if we hadn't gone through that whole journey together, I don't know how Chip and I could ever keep up with the schedule or the pressures brought on by the wonderful opportunities that keep popping up in our lives.

When it comes to success, fame, money, and all those things people think they want in life, I think a lot of us tend to get it backward. This is one of the lessons I'm thankful for learning on the bumpy road we took before landing ourselves on TV.

Most people think that you start off *not* thriving. Then you get a TV show or some other amazing opportunity, you get fame, you get fortune, and *then* you thrive. That's certainly what I thought earlier in my own life. But what's interesting to me is that Chip and I got to a place where we were thriving—as a couple, as a family, as business partners—before any of this new success unfolded.

Our marriage never suffered in all we've gone through because Chip and I were drawn even closer together, knowing down deep in our hearts that we *had* to hold on to each other if we were ever going to make it out alive.

It was in the middle of all that struggle that I found my true inspiration as a designer—the very thing that so many people seem to be drawn to now that I've received this opportunity to share my work with the world.

I always thought that the "thriving" would come when everything was perfect, and what I learned is that it's actually down in the mess that things get good.

It was such a blessing to find myself thriving in the middle of the pain. Unless you find a way to do that, there's always going to be this fake illusion that once you get there—wherever "there" is for you—you'll be happy. But that's just not life. If you can't find happiness in the ugliness, you're not going to find it in the beauty, either.

I have learned that if you're looking for perfection in your house, you can get it. But as soon as you have it, you're going to sit on your couch and find you're still unhappy. You'll find yourself continuing to say, "What's next? What now? What do I need to do?"

I worked hard to try to do it all, to try to live up to the Pinterest perfection that only leaves you discontented. I finally realized that life isn't found on the pages of a magazine—life is found in the glass of spilled milk and in the long, narrow hallway filled with socks and soccer balls.

For the first four years of having kids, I threw elaborate birthday parties. I spent money we shouldn't have spent. And then I realized that my two-year-olds didn't even notice all the details I'd spent so much time and money on. All they wanted was cake! And I did all this for what? For me? To look impressive?

Now I make homemade cakes, I blow up balloons and we pop them. That's all. Kids just want to be kids. They don't obsess about all the details. What they might remember are all the silly faces mom makes when she blows up balloons and the taste of that homemade cake with sprinkles. That's what they'll remember. Not a picture-perfect party.

I had to learn the hard way. I had to go through those kind of "What is my intention behind these things?" questions. I had to go through that feeling that many moms get when the party is over and you're exhausted and mad that you spent all the money before I could share this message with others.

Ready for it? Here it is.

Letting it all go is freeing. (And it's cheaper too!)

I am learning that getting our intentions right simplifies our decisions in life and changes our perspective. And in the end, what it's all about is thankfulness and contentment.

---

In December of 2014, a friend of mine forwarded me a blog post written by a woman who was dying of cancer. Kara Tippetts was thirty-seven years old, and she was in her last months of life as she typed out her post. I'm paraphrasing here, but what she said was, "I'm watching this show in the hospital called *Fixer Upper*, and my kids are at home. I have four kids like them. I wish I could be in my own bed and decorate my house for Christmas."

We were in the middle of filming, working on multiple renovation projects at once, and dealing with the craziness of the holiday season like any other family. But I said, "Chip, I'm going to see her. I feel like I'm supposed to go and decorate her house for Christmas."

We wrote to let her know we were coming, and two close friends of mine hopped on a plane with me to Colorado. When we got to her house, she was upstairs, lying in bed. She had been in the hospital for some time, and she was glad to be home. She was in a lot of pain, but being home with her family gave her comfort.

Kara had lost her hair during chemo and had just started growing it back when I met her. When I walked into her room and saw her for the first time, she radiated so much peace and beauty in the midst of her evident pain. She was so sick that she wasn't supposed to stand up to give me a hug, but she struggled and asked for help and stood up and did it anyway.

"I'm so glad you're here," she said.

Kara's house was chaotic. It was full of life. Full of *her* life. She didn't choose quiet, peaceful, alone time in her final days. She wanted to be in the middle of it all.

I didn't know why I was there. I didn't know what I could do for her. And it turned out, I think, that she did more for me. The more we spoke, the more amazed I was at her story. She chose to find the joy in the midst of suffering. Every inch of her home reflected beauty and life. Before she got sick she had been intentional about celebrating this sweet season of life with four young children—not for anyone else, but her own babies. She had found the secret, and her children thrived there.

I found myself wondering, "What would the world be like if everybody had her mind-set?" She just reconfirmed for me a million times over that it's up to us to choose contentment and thankfulness now—and to stop imagining that we have to have everything perfect before we'll be happy.

I was struggling at that particular time of my life, trying to incorporate the cameras and the long days of filming a TV show around everything else that was going on in our lives. But I left Colorado with an entirely new resolve: I would never forget that all of this is a blessing. I would never forget to be thankful—and to find joy.

Kara passed away a couple of months after our visit. Even though I only visited with her for a couple of days, I felt like I had lost a mentor and dear friend. Her example helped ignite a spark in me to see things differently and to live wholly and intentionally for those closest to me.

I am thankful our show paved a path for me to meet Kara. She was a gift.

People ask us sometimes, "Why the connection? Why are people drawn to *Fixer Upper* and the way you and Chip interact?"

I can't fully answer that question. I honestly don't know. But I think—I hope—that a lot of it has to do with the way we've chosen to live our lives.

And I hope our example is a good one.

# FIFTEEN

# THE BLOOM

In May of 2014, just after the first season of *Fixer Upper* started airing, we did something that had seemed unimaginable eight years earlier. I turned the key in the other direction and reopened my little shop on Bosque Boulevard.

Earlier in January of that same year, Chip and I had traveled to Scottsdale, Arizona, to watch the Baylor Bears play in a national bowl game on New Year's Day. I had a twofold purpose for the trip. I wanted to watch the Bears beat the University of Central Florida with Chip. (Unfortunately the Bears lost, much to Chip's dismay.) And I wanted time to get fresh perspective for the New Year.

It was a beautiful sunny day when Chip dropped me at a park near our hotel. I'd asked him to give me an hour or so to journal and gather my thoughts for the New Year. I found a tree to hide under and I sat there to reflect on the past year. And within moments of sitting down, I heard that voice again. You know the one. That voice said, *It's time to reopen your shop.*

By now you know I like to argue first and then reason later. "Are you serious?" I said out loud. "I have four kids now, a business to run, and a television show. How on earth could I do that?"

But the still, small, oh-so-familiar voice whispered again: *It's time.*

There is always peace when I finally decide to obey that voice.

Although I may wrestle with him at first like a little kid, in the end I always know that he knows best.

I began to get giddy, and I immediately started drawing up a business plan and ideas for my shop's reopening. When Chip arrived to pick me up I walked toward the car, beaming. I opened the door and said, "Chip, it's time to reopen Magnolia."

Of course, in vintage Chip fashion, he responded, "Let's do it!"

Magnolia had outgrown its offices in that space anyway, and had already partially relocated to a larger location. I had a bunch of inventory sitting around that I had planned to use for remodeling projects and staging homes, so it was easy to set it all back up—basically overnight. I had kept in contact with all of my suppliers as well, since I'd continued to do the Magnolia Home shows through the years. It all happened really, really quickly. My regular clientele flocked in as soon as we opened the doors. And because of *Fixer Upper*, new customers started coming in too.

By the middle of 2015, it wasn't unusual for us to see more than a thousand customers a day in that little shop. We had to hire extra help just to stand at the door and control the flow of people in and out so it wouldn't get too crowded for anyone to move in that tiny space. My close friend Jessica (the one from my early shop days) worked at the shop and made it her job to greet every single person who walked in. Her short, pixie-cut hair, bright blue eyes, and glowing smile made every person feel welcome. She was the only employee I had who remembered back when a busy day consisted of fifteen customers.

As we continued to grow, we put up a large temporary tent in the parking lot and put inventory and another cash register in there to try to alleviate the crowding. We even opened an online version of Magnolia Market so that our out-of-town friends could find the things we were selling without having to come to the shop on Bosque. Overnight, it seemed, we had to figure out how to become a shipping company and a business that could cater to thousands of people on a national level.

We rented a mobile container in an attempt to manage all the products people wanted—pillows, signs, those old rusty-looking letters to hang on their walls, candles, you name it—and we ran out of space in a matter of weeks. Then we went looking around for more warehouse space and wound up purchasing an old warehouse that my father used to purchase tires from.

When I walked into the warehouse for the first time, it all came back to me. The smell of tires reminded me of all those years I had sat in my father's tire shop and dreamed about businesses and ideas. God heard my dreams way back then, and this old tire warehouse was confirmation for me that he'd had a plan all along.

In 2015, just to put all of the puzzle pieces in place, we brought my father on to help with operations. Dad had always hoped I would take over his Firestone store. My decision to open Magnolia in 2003 had been hard for him, in fact, because it put an end to his dream of passing his business down to his daughter. But God has a funny way of bringing things back the way only he can do. My dad went from the backbreaking rubber-tire industry to florals and delicate home décor and never skipped a beat.

Chip and I stood back amazed at the number of people who were coming to Waco to visit our little shop. It soon became obvious that we'd need to move the brick-and-mortar Magnolia Market to a bigger location to accommodate the crowds.

---

Anyone driving in or around Waco had probably noticed the pair of big white rusty silos just to the west of Interstate 35. They towered over just about every other structure in town. Located down by the railroad tracks, they were once part of a booming agricultural business. But as long as I'd been aware of them, they had been empty and abandoned.

I had often wondered why that property had stood vacant for so long.

Surely some big hotel or convention center or something would have loved that location—right in the center of everything, close to Baylor, visible from the highway.

My children actually went to school right across the street from those giant old silos. The small building in front, the former office for the operation, had once been a floral shop where Chip would buy me flowers. I loved this building and had taken note years earlier that it had amazing potential. And now that I saw it nearly every day, walking my kids up to the school with those silos towering over us—I found myself even more interested.

One day I dropped the kids off, and as I drove past the silos, I felt like I should turn around and look at the property. My heart was drawn to them the same way it had been stirred when Chip and I drove through the New England coastline on our honeymoon and admired similar old structures.

My first thought that day was, *How convenient to be right next to the kids' school.* I was craving more time with my kids now that they were all in school, and anything to make the commute quicker would ensure more time with my children. I even daydreamed about watching them on the playground from my office.

All of a sudden a business plan came together in my mind as I sat in my car, staring at the property. I envisioned retail space in the grain barn, movie night in the adjacent field, food trucks parked nearby, and maybe a bakery. My mind just flooded with a vision of turning that abandoned cotton-oil mill into Magnolia's new headquarters and retail space—and creating an attraction that could become a whole new center of activity for Waco itself.

The history of this property is what inspired me. I saw this vision of life returning to this once-thriving but now abandoned space. I imagined families and friends coming here and taking a step back in time, putting away their phones, and enjoying the site.

Then I called Chip and told him I wanted to buy it.

"Babe, are you serious? What in the world are we going to do with all that?" he said.

I think after all of the problems we'd endured because of the downturn in the economy and the season of turmoil we had been through, Chip had grown a little more risk averse, a little more cautious. Once again it almost felt like we were switching roles a bit, because I was all-in. I just felt that this was meant to be.

Of course, the property wasn't even for sale, as far as we knew. We didn't know who the owners were at that point or why the property had remained vacant for all those years. But somehow, I just knew it would happen.

It didn't take long for Chip to catch the vision. He tracked down the owner of the property and gave him a call. The owner explained he wasn't interested in selling and that the mill had been his father's business until he passed away in the nineties. He said everyone interested in purchasing the property wanted to tear down the silos, and he did not want that to happen.

Chip assured him the silos were the very things that had drawn us to the property—that instead of removing them, we wanted to highlight them in the downtown area.

I think a lot of people liked seeing them there, whether they thought about it consciously or not. So when we came along and said we wanted to preserve the silos as the landmark they are and to turn this property into something that could serve as a vibrant centerpiece for the whole community, he was interested.

Chip was still skeptical, though. He said, "Jo, this is a big project, and I don't want to get in the same place we were in with the Villas."

"Chip, I just feel like this is right. This is our next step."

Part of me wondered if maybe we could make some money by tearing the giant silos down and selling them for scrap metal. I kept joking with Jo and teasing her about it. But she put together a drawing of the whole space and how she envisioned it coming together. And once I took one look at that, once I truly saw her vision for this retail center and new headquarters for our company, I was 100 percent on board. This place was Jo, no doubt about it.

I just kept thinking back to all those years ago to our honeymoon, how she would have me pull over anytime we'd see silos or an abandoned grain barn. It just made sense, like it was all part of the plan.

I let Chip handle all the negotiations because that's always been his thing. And we were able to make a deal. Once again, just as with the shop on Bosque, just as with the farm we now call home, the seemingly impossible and out of reach became real. In fact, it seemed very meant to be.

Thousands of people showed up when we opened Magnolia Market at the Silos in October of 2015, and they haven't stopped coming ever since. The store has sixteen thousand square feet of floor space, and it's constantly filled with people, inside and out. This rusty old place that some people considered an eyesore is now a viable part of our downtown district. It's also providing jobs to dozens upon dozens of new and long-time Magnolia employees.

Talk about coming full circle. If I ever needed proof that I should trust God with my dreams, this was certainly it. He turned my little dream, my mustard seed of faith, into all this. Not even a decade after I made that difficult decision to close my shop to stay home with my babies, God delivered on the promise of making my dreams come true in ways that were bigger than I ever imagined.

The best part of all of this growth is that we've been able to channel it right back into the town we love. We're both proud of the work our friends and fellow business owners do—the local craftsmen and craftswomen who've dedicated their time and energy to making the beautiful items we showcase, from jewelry to furniture to handmade signs and pottery.

Who knows? Maybe someday soon we'll find a way to bring Magnolia Market to other cities. How cool would it be to feature local artists and craftsmen and to bring this wonderful thing that's happened in our hometown to hometowns all over America?

Look at what Chip unleashed by encouraging me to go open my little shop way back in 2003. Look at what that turned into. I am so grateful for that. I'm not sure if any of these big plans will ever happen, but I sure like to dream about them. And as I've learned, when I speak my dreams out loud to Chip—and to God—those dreams have a way of becoming attainable.

---

Life changes quickly. Overnight, your whole world can change. Chip and I have already experienced that time and time again. And in this season we're in now, which is by far the busiest season of our lives, the changes that have happened are things no one can prepare for.

I'm an introvert by nature. Yet now, everywhere I go, people seem to know me and come up to me and want to talk to me—and it's beautiful. I'm so grateful. And Chip—Chip just loves it. I think he'd like to be president of the United States someday, so he's out there shaking everybody's hand and kissing babies and waving to everybody.

We've simply had to adjust to a new way of living, that's all.

Chip and I both work hard. We continue to make mistakes, and these days we work even harder to learn from them and get better. If I had planned my life, it never would have ended up like this. So maybe it's kind of fun not to plan. Maybe it's more fun just to see where life takes you. After all, we're living proof that sometimes even the messiest stuff and the biggest mistakes can take you someplace wonderful.

Speaking of which, we finally sold that old houseboat. We never did get it in the water. That thing just sat there until the summer of

2015, when we finally found a buyer who was willing to devote the time and energy that boat needed to come back to life.

I was mad at Chip when he bought that houseboat. I think I had every right to be mad. But the point is that it turned out okay. It turned out better than okay. That stupid houseboat was the catalyst that got us to where we are now.

And no, the dream isn't about fame and fortune. For me, the dream is that I get to wake up every morning and do what I love with the ones I love.

When Chip is out in the field herding the goats or working the cows, he gets that same feeling—because back when he was little he said to himself, "One day I want to do what my granddad does."

Being on a farm is something we both dreamed about, and in the hustle and bustle of our busy life, when I come back here to this place I love, it always takes me back to the basics. That's why I go into that garden and I work with my hands. That's why I think it's important that Chip works with those animals. There's something about doing things the way our ancestors used to do them that kind of puts your heart back into the rhythm of this thing called life. It's why I think cooking for my family is important. It's why I love making things with my hands, designing with my hands, and gardening with my hands.

I think it's important to reiterate here that I didn't start out wanting to be a gardener, or a designer for that matter. It was *all* trial and error and figuring things out. And sometimes you've got to try something outside of your comfort zone to figure out what it is that you truly love.

Well, you could say that about you and me right from the start. You were never looking for the loud guy, and I certainly wasn't looking for the quiet girl.

Now I look back and go, "If I would've ended up with that quiet guy or that stable guy or that safe guy, I would never have been able to pursue any of these dreams, because no one would have pushed me to these new places I discovered in myself." Those other types of guys might have allowed me to stay in that safe place.

They wouldn't have drawn you out. That's interesting. And if I had wound up with some cheerleader who was always the life of the party, I don't think I would have found my way, either. I needed you for that.

Nowadays when I think about the name *Magnolia*, I think about it in terms that refer to much more than the blossoming of our business. I think about the buds on the tree, and how they really are just the tightest buds—they look like rocks, almost. And I feel like when Chip and I met, that tight little bud was *me*. I was risk averse, and in some ways, I don't think I saw the beauty or the potential in myself. Then I wound up with Chip Gaines and—

You bloomed?

I did. If I hadn't married Chip, I might not have ever bloomed.

I can't imagine what my life would be if we hadn't traveled this road. We celebrated our twelfth anniversary recently, and my dad said something that I thought was really beautiful. He said, "Chip, I always thought, when I was out on the baseball field hitting you those grounders, that I was training you to be the next greatest baseball player. But now, looking back and seeing the person you've become, I was really training you to be the next greatest dad."

We've both spent a lot of time attempting to figure out what it is we love so much about life on the farm and also why so many other people who watch our show seem drawn to it too. And what it comes down to is this: A farm is what inspired the both of us from the very beginning. It's what inspired Chip as a young kid. It's what inspired me as a young girl, in my daydreaming. And now we're living our dream. We found our way to this place we love through all sorts of twists and turns and bumps and forks in the road. But we're here.

It isn't as if we're trying to push our lifestyle on anyone. If we're trying to push anything, it's the hope that there's contentment in the journey. Whether you are in an eight-hundred-square-foot home or living in a dream house on a lake, contentment is found on the *way* to the "farm," not on the "farm" itself.

We both hope, with all of our hearts, that the people who read this book and watch our show and come to see what we're working on in Waco will take a chance to go after their dreams too. Because the key to everything Chip and I have learned in our life together so far seems to be pretty simple: Go and find what it is that inspires you, go and find what it is that you love, and go do that until it hurts.

Don't quit, and don't give up. The reward is just around the corner. And in times of doubt or times of joy, listen for that still, small voice. Know that God has been there from the beginning—and he will be there until . . .

The End.

# ABOUT THE AUTHORS

**Chip** was born in Albuquerque, New Mexico and was raised in Dallas, Texas. He graduated from Baylor University's Hankamer School of Business with a degree in marketing. Chip is an entrepreneur by nature, and started and sold many small businesses before Magnolia. Having grown up spending time on his granddad's ranch in North Texas, Chip became a true cowboy at heart. He was made for hard labor and always preferred digging ditches to academic pursuits.

**Joanna**, also known by friends and fans as "Jo" or "JoJo," was born in Kansas and raised in the Lone Star State. She graduated from Baylor University with a degree in communications and was inspired to join the world of design while interning in New York City. Joanna decided to open a home decor shop, Magnolia Market, in 2003; bringing her NYC-inspired ideas and eye for design back to Waco, Texas. She soon discovered this passion complemented Chip's construction experience, and together they began remodeling and flipping homes.

**Mark Dagostino** is a multiple *New York Times* bestselling co-author whose career has been built through the sharing of uplifting and inspirational life stories. Before becoming an author, he served ten years on staff in New York and LA as a well-respected correspondent, columnist, and senior writer for *People* magazine, sharing powerful interviews with many diverse personalities. Today, he lives a somewhat quieter life in New Hampshire—in a home that he really wishes Chip and Jo would come fix up!

*we would love to*
SEE YOU AT THE SILOS,
UNTIL THEN YOU CAN VISIT US AT

MAGNOLIAMARKET.COM